D1207402

Barbara

THE UNCONSCIOUS AUTOBIOGRAPHY OF A CHILD GENIUS

The University of North Carolina Press
Chapel Hill

Barbara

THE UNCONSCIOUS AUTOBIOGRAPHY OF A CHILD GENIUS

EDITED BY HAROLD GRIER McCURDY

IN COLLABORATION WITH HELEN FOLLETT

FOREWORD

How do we read a human life? As a series of disconnected accidents or as the unfolding of a drama with an inner unity? Anyone we know appears to us at some instant of time with a history we do not know and may never know, or know only in fragments, and in most cases after short acquaintance disappears from our view into a veiled future. Moreover, much that is of great personal concern occurs secretly, in wishes and dreams that are never expressed. Biographies fascinate us because they promise a more sweeping panorama of an individual life than our ordinary day-to-day contacts permit. Yet a biography does not necessarily provide us with a meaningful, comprehensible unity; it may seem to confirm the opinion that life is a series of accidents. For the unity of a life, if it exists, is a matter of an individual myth, to borrow a phrase from Thomas Mann; and we may not know this myth. To know it we have to start far back in the individual history and know those things which children know and do not as a rule articulate very fully, and we have to be in at the death. Act One in a good drama enables us to understand Act Five, it prepares us for it, but riddlingly: not because the foreshadowings of Act One are vague, but because we do not perceive them clearly for what they are, or do not believe them, until Act Five has clarified and confirmed them. And so we need Act Five to comprehend Act One.

To a greater degree than usual the life of Barbara Newhall Follett (1914–1939), daughter of the authors Wilson Follett (1887–1963) and Helen Thomas Follett, meets these demands and justifies the proposition that an individual life is the unfolding of a quite individual drama. As a child of four in New England she was already seated at a typewriter expressing her dreams. By thirteen she had published a book with Knopf, *The House Without Windows*, which concentratedly summed up some of the major aspects of these inner truths and which was acclaimed by critics like Howard Mumford Jones for its literary qualities. And by twenty-five, on a December evening in 1939, she had stepped out of her apartment in Boston and had vanished from the world, as completely and mysteriously as the heroine of that book, who had been crowned queen of the fairies high among the mountain snows and was then carried away by butterflies.

It detracts not at all from the inner cogency of the drama that it took place in the midst of events on a large public scale, such as the great economic depression of 1929 and the threatening postures of Hitler in Europe, which might conceivably have affected the young woman that she then was; or that she poignantly felt the shock of her father's separation from the family, which, coinciding with the Great Depression, might be held sufficient to account for much that followed. One cannot say that these and other external events did nothing to shape the drama. But one can say that long before they happened in their particularity not only had the main lines of the drama been laid down but the future had in some degree, even in an uncanny degree, been specified; so that the external events were at least as much demanded by the drama as productive of it.

My first knowledge of Barbara came through a letter from Mrs. Follett, her mother, about an article of mine touching on the problem of genius. Because of the bearing of this article on Mrs. Follett's letter I will state that in it I concluded, from biographical study of twenty noted men, that their intellectual development seemed to have been promoted by a combination of three factors: (1) intense stimulation by adults, usually loving, who were concerned with their intellectual development, (2) relative isolation during childhood from other children, and (3) considerable exercise of the imagination. I remarked that this combination of factors was not such as to be favored by our public school system, and I commented also that genius was in some cases a costly gift, as exemplified in some of the men of genius I had examined. My article, entitled "The Childhood Pattern of Genius," appeared originally in 1957 in the *Journal of the Elisha Mitchell Scientific Society* and was reprinted in 1959 in the Smithsonian Institution's 1958 *Annual Report*; and thereupon, to my great surprise, made newspaper headlines early in 1960. A flood of mail instantly followed. Among the letters I valued was the one I have mentioned. Under the date, March 14, Mrs. Follett wrote, in part:

Your study of childhood patterns of genius as summarized in the N. Y. Times of Jan. 6, 1960 attracted my attention for a special reason that I think may interest you. To state it simply, I have in my possession what I believe is a case study (possibly a unique one), voluminously documented, that seems to fulfill the high points of your thesis.

This documentation consists of a child's own writings from about the age of four through a ten- or twelve-year period. Mostly, it is in type-written form, the child having appropriated the small typewriter at an early age as a useful tool for her avid desire to express herself in words.

There is in this collection a vast amount of prose and poetry (fact, fiction, fantasy), whichever mode of expression suited the demands of her ever-expanding imagination. And—what may be of the greatest importance—are the hundred or more personal letters the child wrote to friends (three adults in particular over an extended period of years).

These letters were returned at a later date, the recipients believing them to be of documentary value.

If anyone is interested in tracing the development of one child's imagination as it went joyously, restlessly, often discontentedly on its way, a perusal of this child's own writings would reveal some of the hundreds of details that fed and animated her questing, creative spirit. There came a moment of satisfaction, I believe, when the child's fancy came to fruition, taking form and pattern in a small book, called "The House Without Windows," published in 1927 by Knopf.

Howard Mumford Jones (Professor Jones was, I believe, at Chapel Hill at the time) in his review of "The House Without Windows" spoke of the author as a child genius. He wrote in part: the book was "the profoundest revelation of a child's fondness for beauty yet in American prose . . . a lyric artist. She writes as though she were living in that serene abode where the eternal are . . . that is where she lives and where she takes us. . . ."

Professor Jones adds: "The author has never been to school. There seems to be no sane reason why she should ever go to one, unless she wants to. . . ."

Whether this child-author would have come under your classification "genius" I don't know. A costly gift, if so, as you pointed out. Whether this young writer should have gone to school is something to ponder about (as you suggest) in terms of gains and losses. But that she had literary talent can hardly be doubted, although one wonders whether it should have been curbed or allowed to run riot. A happy medium, perhaps?

Your article re-awakened my interest in the whole matter of creativity and the child, together, I must admit, with many current essays on the subject and the complaints of educators against too much "conformity." And I am wondering if a selection of these documents, accompanied by an editorial comment from a competent person in this field of education, would be of any help to parents, teachers, and psychologists, would even serve, perhaps, as a warning.

As for myself, I am neither a psychologist nor a teacher. I am a more or less retired writer, who, as a parent, has retained a lively interest in today's children and their education. I live in the neighborhood of Columbia University and am accessible to anyone (and with pleasure); and to anyone concerned with the matter referred to, I would add a special welcome.

To this generous letter I promptly replied on March 19:

I enclose a copy of the study to which you referred. As you will see, it is strictly empirical and leaves the difficult "value judgments" up in the air. Nevertheless, the problem is there: the conformity pressures of the school system and the peer group vs. the full burden of intense individuality. On top of this, I think that we are very ignorant (I mean myself) about all that is involved in any human life, whether conforming or non-conforming, whether apparently happy or apparently tragic. I feel that we move about in the midst of towering realities which we do not understand, and that it is quite impossible for us to judge the significance of any individual career. Whether a life is long or short, famous or obscure, I feel that it has its place, its meaning, in the whole, and that it reaches out infinitely beyond human apprehension.

So, for me, every person is unique and mysterious. Yet there are some persons who display this mystery more luminously than others. We are especially in their debt. It seems to me that the documents you described might indeed enrich us. Perhaps, with the annotations you suggest, they would serve more as a revelation than as a warning—a revelation of the extraordinary possibilities, both dark and bright, in a single little girl. For you hint at tragedy, the costliness of the gift. Yet it is difficult for me to believe that the tragedy was not shot through with a very lovely brilliance, or you could not remember her as you do.

Perhaps you will be willing to tell me more. In the meantime, I have sent off for a copy of "The House Without Windows." Please let me hear from you again, if you are so disposed. It may be that we could arrange a meeting eventually. My wife and son and I expect to be in New York a day or so before sailing for Europe in early June.

In June, before leaving for Europe, I made a short afternoon call on Mrs. Follett, with my wife and son. It was evident from her reticence as well as from the few things she told me that it cost her something to remember her lost child. Nevertheless, I encouraged her to go through her daughter's writings leading up to *The House Without Windows* (a quite remarkable book, as I had discovered) and offered to help her put them in order, as a perhaps unique case history in the development of a writer's imagination. My own daughter had died two years before, and grief made me bold. Later, in our unhurried progress through Barbara's writings, through the windings of her imagination and the events of her external life, we agreed that we should go beyond the halfway point originally set—the high point of *The House Without Windows*—and follow, even down painful declivities, the remainder of her life to its mysterious end.

With this agreement we were passing beyond a study of the literary development of a child author into a full-length, though still strictly limited, biography. On both sides, but particularly on Mrs. Follett's, was a desire to hold references to other persons to a minimum and keep them as anonymous as possible. Again on both sides, but particularly on mine, was the aim to tell a life story from the inside, from the point of view of the one living it—which, with Barbara, meant telling it through stories and poems of hers even more than through her letters. We had no desire to gossip, much less to wound anyone. By keeping very close to Barbara's own words and by emphasizing the imaginative writings, and by centering our attention on her personality and the meaning of events rather than on details of history (especially other people's history), we hoped to convey the essentials of a vivid life with discretion and with full respect for every person involved in it. We should be dismayed if it seemed otherwise. Mrs. Follett has chosen to keep even herself very much in the background, and I think that, quite apart from every other consideration, it is in harmony with our way of presenting Barbara that she should do so. Nevertheless, she is willing for the reader to know (what it may be useful for the reader to know) that she undertook to conduct Barbara's education at home rather then send her to school, in order to allow her full intellectual individuality to flourish under a schedule of work that grew naturally out of the child's interests and preferred ways of inquiry and expression. The home was rich in literary and artistic and general intellectual resources, and other cultivated adults besides the parents gave their attention to the little girl. She responded to this loving care by enthusiastically learning and creating. It was a part of Mrs. Follett's educational philosophy that mastery of the English language as an expressive medium was a basic accomplishment, and she discovered that a typewriter was a more convenient writing tool for a small child than a pen or pencil. By eight years of age Barbara had this instrument under perfect control. Present-day researchers into the uses of the typewriter as an educational device for the very young should be aware of Mrs. Follett's pioneering work. They could profit by reading her article, "Education à la Carte," in the *Pictorial Review* for July, 1929.

At my request Mrs. Follett has written down some of her recollections of the home and circumstances in which Barbara received her education, for use in this Foreword. I select from her brief memoir the portions that supply details not to be distinctly found in the text of our book—details, in fact, which in their explicitness are new to me at this moment. The account begins:

Both parents, after graduation from separate colleges, became teachers; I, myself, a High School teacher until marriage, and the child's father a college teacher in the English department of a New England Uni-

versity. A small salary, a modest home, one with a pleasant atmosphere with its early American furniture (my mother's), many books, a friend's piano and music to suit an assortment of tastes—such was the scene that the child was soon to know in its every detail.

A lively gathering-place our home was at tea-time. Students and young Faculty came; sometimes a well-known author or musician. Always plenty of talk and animated discussion. Here, among the guests, the barely four-year-old made frequent appearances. Then, bored, she would run upstairs to the quieter sanctum of her grandmother's room, and into the waiting arms of her dearly loved grandmother.

About the same time, and in the midst of these happy family surroundings, the small Barbara became acquainted with the small typewriter. Used to seeing it on my desk, and hearing its staccato noise, she was determined one day to investigate this mysterious Thing. And I was there to explain. Entranced that her own fingers could make the keys jump, creating strange marks on a piece of paper, and a bell ring, she resolved, then and there, so I believe, to make that odd Thing her own. The moment of contact with what would become the most valuable tool in her life, was at hand. Almost at once the story related in this book began to take form, though unsuspected for years to come.

Suddenly, it seemed, everything became bigger—a bigger city and University; a bigger salary and house, and a bigger circle of friends. The little girl accepted them all quite naturally, so long as her basic needs were there—her family. Now there were neighbors close by, and Barbara found playmates of her own size. They climbed trees and played games, and often visited each other's homes. Sometimes, a parent took them all to a puppet show, to the museum, or to a children's concert. Delighted as she was to be a part of this group, Barbara was also happy to be alone with her animal friends who sat around in chairs while she read one of her favorite stories, found in Kipling's Jungle Book, to her attentive audience.

Her father was her very special outdoor companion. And Saturday was the day. Then they would take long walks together, and talk about everything from the snake they might find in the grass to spring flowers and sunsets. They talked about books and Barbara was encouraged to read Dickens as his students were doing. Only, she would have her father to help her. Later by a year or two, there came canoeing and mountain-climbing trips that they shared together. A lifelong devotion of each to the other was a promise that needed no words.

nimal friends to whom Barbara read The Jungle Book

It should be explained that her father, Wilson Follett, after a decade of teaching English at Dartmouth, Brown, and Harvard, became an editor at the Yale University Press and then at Knopf. Skipping over a part of Mrs. Follett's account that refers to adult friends whom the book that follows sufficiently describes, I extract another very informative passage:

Making a closer scrutiny of this educational experience is necessary, I believe, so that it may not be thought of as a happy-go-lucky affair, lacking method and discipline. Each day a schedule was made out that roughly corresponded with that of the early grades of the school system: arithmetic, geography, science, reading, arts and crafts, music, and the beginning of French. A week's work divided up as we thought best. Added to each day's studies came that of typing for ten or twenty minutes which meant, at first, the copying of words and sentences, and later, the composing of sentences of her own.

The regret (or blessing?) was that I couldn't watch the details of this schooling idea taking place on a small table presided over by a small girl on a sunny porch. It was my part to make out the schedules, and her part to carry them out, clip her papers together, and then bounce outdoors to find a playmate for the afternoon. As a housewife I could never call my work finished. The child had, I think, the best of the bargain, for she learned the good habit of working alone, with occasional calls for help. And with broom or dustcloth in hand, I was glad to answer.

The years slipped by: the family included a new baby—a sister whom we thought of as a gift to Barbara, whose happiness now seemed complete. So proud was this nine-year-old Barbara that a new radiance appeared to surround her in a shining world of her imagination that lovingly embraced her baby sister. Her stories, in pencil, or typed, surged with a new-found creativeness, and gave great pleasure and amusement to her family that now became her favorite audience.

Here I skip another section, chiefly concerned with Barbara's development as a user of words, and come to this concluding paragraph:

At last, High School loomed up as a new experience, and Barbara looked forward to it with a certain amount of pleasure, and an ample amount of curiosity. She was well prepared, her home schooling having met, in its own way, the basic requirements. Suddenly, however, Fate stepped in, and turned the young girl's life in a strangely different direction, one for which she was totally unprepared.

Although I sympathize with her meaning, I cannot entirely agree with Mrs. Follett in her last remark, which refers to Wilson Follett's break with his family in 1928, when his wife and two young daughters were living in New Haven and he was spending most of his time in New York on his editorial job with Knopf. I do not think that Barbara was totally unprepared for this turn of events. Her writings, even at an early age, bear traces of the future in them; her life has a continuity of great tensile strength. So it seems to me, looking at it in retrospect through a stranger's eyes; and yet not a stranger either, having been intimate with her imagination. I have fancied that one totally uninformed about her, as I was when I first became acquainted with *The House Without Windows*, might have been able to infer from her childhood letters, poems, and fairy tales the events to come, if set resonating to the inner harmonies and disharmonies of those writings. Perhaps it is a mere fancy; and yet, so it seems in retrospect. Our weakness is that we ordinarily do not take the expressions of a person's innermost life quite seriously enough. "This is a fairy tale," we say. "It is written by a child," we say. "The writer is *our* child, our old acquaintance, someone we understand perfectly." And so we miss the essential truth, gay or sad, which the expression contains, and especially its significance for the future. Afterwards, if we have been involved in the drama and it is tragic, we may blame ourselves. We may see ourselves, or someone else, as the cause of consequences we think we might have prevented. There, too, we are in danger of being mistaken. In arrogating to ourselves such responsibility we may only be continuing to avoid awareness of the flaw with which we may truly be chargeable—a stubborn blindness to the fact of individual existence. I mean the fact that the other person is indeed not ourselves, that what the other expresses is a reality not centered in us, whatever pleasure or pain it may bring us.

It has been my purpose in these five years of collaboration with Mrs. Follett, so often broken into and interrupted for long periods by different concerns, to help her set forth from the materials at her disposal a true account of Barbara—for our own clarification first of all, and then, if it seemed fitting, for the clarification of others. It has seemed fitting, and we now publish this essay in biography for any who may want to broaden their sympathies by participation in a life not their own, but unique and real as theirs. My hope is that readers will come to this book not looking for abstract formulas or explanations—least of all, psychoanalytic explanations—but in a mood susceptible to the quick flitting or slow throbbing of butterfly wings.

Harold G. McCurdy

Chapel Hill, N.C.
February 1, 1966

Illustrations

Barbara

THE UNCONSCIOUS AUTOBIOGRAPHY OF A CHILD GENIUS

Chapter I

By five years of age most children have asked the big questions. Few of them, however, have begun to write the answers. Barbara had—because she could type.

Her first important correspondent was an elderly Swedish gentleman who restored antiques. They met in his shop in Providence when she was four. She was carrying a stuffed toy rabbit who had lost an eye. Mr. Oberg took sympathetic notice and paused in his work on two ancient clocks to repair the deficiency in her rabbit. She was impressed. Not long afterwards she composed a story in Mr. Oberg's honor, and signed it with her full name:

Twelve clocks were on a shelf all ticking away.

They wanted to take a walk, so they Jumped down and started.

A little dog saw them and pushed one over, then another, and finally all.

They were broken into pieces. Then Mr. Oberg came along and said: "Oh my!" and put the pieces into a basket and took them home. He mended them; and now they are as good as new.

Barbara Newhall Follett *

Since many things are broken in this world—some by naughty dogs, some by children, some by the Forces—it is good to know a Mr. Oberg who can mend them.

Barbara knew other people, of course. A month later (it was April, 1919, and she had turned five in March) she was writing from

* Spelling errors and typographical deviations are extremely rare in Barbara's writings, even at four and five years of age. Most of the few that do exist have been allowed to stand. Very occasionally a correction has been introduced to keep the reader from stumbling. Here and there in the letters a personal reference has been deleted or disguised, or slightly altered for the sake of intelligibility. In short, there has been a minimum of editorial tampering with the manuscript materials, and none of it has been for the purpose of "touching up" the image of Barbara, either as a writer or as a person.

Cheshire, Connecticut, to her grown-up Cousin Helen in Boston, *"Please come to see me this summer so we can go and pick butter-cups and try to catch butterflies."* There were Mother and Father and grandmother Ding, too; and birds and flowers; and also snakes. In July she wrote to Mr. Oberg:

The goldfinches come every afternoon and eat their supper on the clump of bachelor's-buttons right on the left-hand side of the path that leads from the back door to our road. There are ten gold-finches, five males and five females. Before they eat their suppers, they sit on the clothesline and swing in the breeze. I wish you could be here to see them.

Day before yesterday Daddy killed a snake in the potato-patch; then he threw the snake away with a stick, and then he threw away the stick. The next day Ding and I went down Ridgeview Place, and there were the snake and the stick. The snake was about three feet long.

Grandfather Bunny has lost his right eye, and I stuck in a black and a blue pin.

One day last week Ding and I went down to the orchard and sat among the brown-eyed Susans and had a picnic. I took two Bolivar cookies and some bread-and-butter sandwiches in my lunch-bas-ket.

We have some enormous pink hollyhocks in the flower-garden, and lots of white ones. A few of the flowers have gone to seed, but new ones are coming all the time.

Yet though in this world clocks stop, bunnies lose their eyes, flowers go to seed, snakes are killed, and the snake-killer himself breaks his kite when he tries to fly it (as she records in A *Little Book of Clocks and Things*), there is plenty of gaiety too:

"One foot, two feet!" sang the tree,
Dancing, dancing in glee;
"Ripple, ripple!" sang the brook,
Rushing through a little nook

—as she wrote later in the month. To be sure, there is motion in this gaiety, and motion is kin to running, and running is kin to running away. "The Kitty That Ran Away" is the title of a story written in September:

ONCE upon a time Ding and I went out for a walk in the orchard to get some apples. While we were there we saw a little kitty up in a hole in a tree. When we reached home we met Mother and Daddy and told them all about the kitty. Then Daddy took Jean and me down to the orchard again to try to find the kitty; we found it but we did not catch it.

Later in September she has a request, as well as thanks, for Mr. Oberg, the restorer of lost and broken things:

Please come back with Mother and Daddy.
Thank you very much for Peter, the painting-book, and the little animal eyes for Grandfather Bunny and Peter.

A rhymed couplet in October puts the loveliness and evanescence of the world in twelve words:

Watch the clouds move all day
And shadows come and go away.

In view of all the uncertainties, one surely needs a dependable, snuggly creature to cuddle up to. Barbara can rejoice, December 20, in red and black type:

I have a little Peter Bunny;
I love him, he is so very funny.

And also:

Dear little Bunny,
    Come to me—
Dear little Bunny,
    Full of glee!

If now we add to the cast of characters a brown rocking-horse which Barbara received on her fifth birthday, and a spinning-wheel which entered the family during the year, we are almost prepared for her first long story, worked at intermittently for several months before she was six. We need only to be reminded that, for children, everything in the world is alive or can easily become so, and that magic is normal.

The Life of the Spinning-Wheel, the Rocking-Horse, and the Rabbit

Chapter I

Once upon a time, though I can't say exactly when, there lived in a far-off country a spinning-wheel, a rocking-horse, and a rabbit. They knew many of the people in that country. They lived in a house with many pretty things in it, such as I am going to tell you about: amethysts, turquoises, opals, pearls, diamonds, and rubies, and precious stones of all kinds.

One day when Mrs. Spinning-Wheel had her head stretched out of her window looking down upon the glorious garden of flowers, she was saying to herself, humming a low, sweet little song,—"Oh dear! how I wish Mr. Horse were white!"

Mr. Rabbit was hiding in a corner behind the door, and he heard what Mrs. Spinning-Wheel had said. "Ha! Ha!" said Mr. Rabbit to Mrs. Spinning-Wheel, with a wiggle of his nose, "Mr. Horse shall be white, as white as you want him to be."

"Eh?" replied Mrs. Spinning-Wheel.

"I say" began Mr. Rabbit a little louder. But Mrs. Spinning-Wheel interrupted him, saying:

"What do you mean to say to me?"

"I mean to say to you," said Mr. Rabbit, "that Mr. Horse shall be as white as you want him to be."

"Ah! now I get you," said Mrs. Spinning-Wheel, with a merry little laugh. "But," said she, in a few minutes, "how are you going to make Mr. Horse as white as snow?"

"I am going to take a fairy's wand," said Mr. Rabbit to Mrs. Spinning-Wheel.

"A bright idea!" exclaimed she.

"Well then," said Mr. Rabbit, "tomorrow morning I'll go off for the wand. But now Mrs. Clock says seven and so I should think we might as well go to bed."

And so they all went to bed.

Chapter II

The next day the sun shone through the trees, and warmed the flowers, in their garden. The sun had dried them after the rain had drenched them. How irridescent they were with the sun shining through the drops of rain that hadn't dried up! The flowers bloomed sweet and fresh. How glad they were to have the morning sun shine on them! I will now tell you what kind of flowers there were in Mrs. Spinning-Wheel's garden: dahlias, lilies, pansies, bachelor's-buttons, and yellow sunflowers higher than her head. (As it happened Mrs. Spinning-Wheel was taller than the other two of them.) There were some wild flowers in that country, also: violets, wild sunflowers, buttercups, daisies, and just a few dandelions. Most of them had gone by because it was nearly autumn, and they had all gone out into those little fuzzy balls that children like to blow out.

After the family had had their breakfast, Mr. Rabbit said to Mrs. Spinning-Weel: "Mrs. Spinning-Weel, I think that I will now put on my things and go to fetch that fairy-wand. Goodbye."

"Goodbye," answered Mrs. Spinning-Wheel, I shall be sorry to have you leave me.

"But," said Mr. Rabbit, "you must remember that it will take me quite a long time to get the fairy-wand."

"Oh," said Mrs. Spinning-Wheel, I could wait forever if I knew that Mr. Horse was going to be white sometime." As it happened, Mr. Horse was a dark brown.

"Well," said Mr. Rabbit, "I don't think that you could wait quite forever."

So Mr. Rabbit took down from a peg a fur coat which had been given to him by Mrs. Spinning-Wheel, and he took a woolly cap out of the cupboard where he kept things, and he took a little box to carry the wand in. After carefully saying "Goodbye," again to Mrs. Spinning-Wheel, he hurried out the door and soon disappeared down the path that led to the forest.

By and by he met a fairy with two wands in her hand, and he asked her why she had two wands?

The fairy evidently knew his name because she said to him: "Good day to you, my dear Mr. Rabbit, I have two wands because one of them is for you to keep always for yourself."

"Oh no!", said Mr. Rabbit, "you'll want it yourself."

"No, no, take it," said the kind fairy.

"I thank you," said Mr. Rabbit politely, "that is the very thing that I came into the woods for."

"What do you want it for?" said the fairy.

"I want it because Mr. Horse is brown, and Mrs. Spinning-Wheel wants him white. I want to do what she wishes, you know."

"Yes, I know," said the fairy, in her softest voice.

So Mr. Rabbit put the wand which she had given him into the box and ran home to tell Mrs. Spinning-Wheel about it.

When he reached home he found Mrs. Spinning-Wheel sitting on the sofa in the living-room putting the jewels into rings. Mr. Horse had four amethyst ones, and Mrs. Spinning-Wheel herself had four turquoise ones, and Mr. Rabbit had all the rest.

There was a hole in the box that Mr. Rabbit had the wand in, and Mrs. Spinning-Wheel saw the star of the wand shining through it; so by that she knew that he had succeeded in getting the wand.

"Hello Mr. Rabbit, so you have returned again, have you? That's good. I know you have succeeded in getting the wand for I see something shining in your box; I'm pleased to know that you had good luck," said Mrs. Spinning-Wheel gaily.

Then Mr. Rabbit took the wand out of the box and touched Mr. Horse with it. Immediately Mr. Horse was snow white.

"Well, well Mr. Rabbit," said Mr. Horse, I ain't brown any more, am I? Ain't you a smart rabbit to do all this! It don't seem natural to be white, but then I've always wanted to be that color.

"Doesn't Mr. Horse talk bad grammar," muttered Mr. Rabbit to himself.

Just then one of the up-stairs windows opened and Mrs. Spinning-Wheel put her head out. When she saw the white horse she jumped with joy, saying: "Oh Mr. Horse is white, oh Mr. Horse is white; I jump for joy, I jump for joy."

Then Mr. Rabbit looked up and saw Mrs. Spinning-Wheel's bright face, and he said to her: "Mr. Horse talks very bad grammar."

"Yes he does; I've noticed that," said Mrs. Spinning-Wheel. The next minute Mr. Rabbit and Mr. Horse noticed that Mrs. Spinning-Wheel's bright face was gone. She came rushing out of the house like a train of cars without either hat or coat on, and she jumped on the back of Mr. Horse and rode round the yard.

Mr. Horse was angry about that for he did not like to have people on his back. So angry was he that he threw her off Swunk! onto the leaves.

The same fairy that had given Mr. Rabbit the wand was hiding behind an old apple-tree and saw what Mr. Horse had done. She ran out from behind the tree, touched Mrs. Spinning-Wheel with her wand, and in an instant she was standing upright, and she saw that it was getting dark. So they all went in the house, undressed themselves, and all snuggled down in their beds and were soon fast asleep.

Chapter III

The next morning the sun rose high in the sky and the shadows ran swiftly everywhere. The sky was a clear, cloudless blue. That summer Mrs. Spinning-Wheel had planted a double row of sunflowers on each side of the path that led down their front lawn and into the forest. Six o'clock struck, but Mrs. Spinning-Wheel was sound asleep all the time and did not hear it strike. Seven o'clock struck, but she did not hear that, either. But when eight o'clock struck, she heard it and jumped out of bed. She went to the window that looked down upon those lovely sunflowers, and put out her head and looked at them.

Soon breakfast was prepared, and as Mr. Horse always cooked every meal, breakfast, dinner, supper, he rang the bell. . Up started Mrs. Spinning-Wheel and like a wild deer she hurried down-stairs. When she reached the bottom of the stairs, she found Mr. Horse and Mr. Rabbit already seated at the table; Mr. Rabbit was eating carrots, while Mr. Horse was feasting on oats; and Mrs. Spinning-Wheel joined in and feasted on Post-Toasties and one or two jelly sandwiches.

After they had eaten their fill, Mrs. Spinning-Wheel said to Mr. Rabbit: "Don't you think it's time you took that wand back to the fairy again? I don't think that she would be so kind as to give you her wand. I think she must be joking."

"Well," said Mr. Rabbit, wiggling his nose, "perhaps she is: I was thinking about that my-self. I believe I will run over and find out."

So Mr. Rabbit dressed himself up in his warmest out-door clothes, just as he did before when he went to get the wand, took the wand in his hand and away he rushed helter-skelter into the forest.

When he came to the place where he had met the fairy before, he saw no sign of her. So he wandered on through the forest until he came to a large oak tree under which he sat down to rest. But he did not see her then, either.

So he walked on and on until he got clearly two miles from home. But he wasn't frightened at all, no indeed, not a brave rabbit like him. By and by he came to a tiny peach-tree on a branch of which he noticed that a large yellow butterfly with black spots on his wings was resting. The minute this wonderful thing that used to be a caterpillar crawling on weeds recognized Mr. Rabbit, he spread his wings and away he flew, circling higher and higher up into the air until he reached the topmost branch of the tallest forest tree.

Mr. Rabbit sat down under the peach-tree to rest; his eyelids drooped, and in a minute he fell fast asleep. When he awoke he thought he heard a swooping of wings, and he looked above him to see whose they could be. But when he looked up he could see nothing. So on and on he went until, when he got almost two miles and one half from home, he came to a large oak tree shedding acorns in the wind, and over that he could see a large ball with wings of all colors was flying toward the west. The colors in it were emerald, amethyst, turquoise, diamond, and ruby.

It was the fairy that Mr. Rabbit had come into the woods for. She had curled herself up into a ball; all fairies do for that is the only way they can fly. Mr. Rabbit knew all this, and he discovered that it was she. Soon as she saw the wand she circled down lower and lower until she alighted on the top of the oak tree. She called to Mr. Rabbit from her perch on the tree. She said to him: "Mr. Rabbit, I wasn't joking; the wand is yours. And did you make Mr. Horse white?"

"Yes, I did," answered Mr. Rabbit.

"I am certainly glad of it," said the fairy. Then she uncurled herself, and said to him: "Hush, Mr. Rabbit, keep still, I hear a roaring sound. It sounds like this: R-r-r-r-r R-R-R-R-R. Let us run and hide."

"I thank you, kind fairy," said Mr. Rabbit, "but I must go home to Mrs. Spinning-Wheel and Mr. Horse, now. Goodbye."

"Goodbye," repeated the fairy.

The roaring seemed to grow louder, and that meant that the beast that made the roaring was coming nearer to them. Anyway, the fairy curled herself up into a ball and away she flew into her house and hid behind the door. Mr. Rabbit scampered away as fast as his fours could carry him; he hurried into his own house to tell his brother and sister about it. Evidently they both knew what the roaring meant. I cannot tell you how Mr. Horse happened to know what it meant, but he did; and Mrs. Spinning-Wheel knew because he had told her.

Mrs. Spinning-Wheel brought Mr. Horse's word to Mr. Rabbit, and told him exactly what made the roaring. "It is a lion," said she. And they all trembled.

After they had all stopped trembling, Mr. Rabbit told them what to do. He said to them: "you two must get quickly into your beds, and I will go down to the door, and when the lion comes in I will prevent him from eating you two up."

So Mrs. Spinning-Wheel and Mr. Horse both got into Mrs. Spinning-Wheel's bed. Every night she and Mr. Rabbit slept together, but this time Mr. Horse cuddled up beside her because his bed was made up and he didn't care to take the trouble to take off the spread. Also he was in a great hurry for he feared that the lion would come in, he was so very near the house.

When Mr. Rabbit saw them safe in bed he went down to the

front door. He opened it, and heard the bad Mr. Lion's loud roaring again. But he didn't see him. I say "bad" because Mr. Lion was bad for he came there to eat them up.

So long as Mr. Rabbit didn't see Mr. Lion at the front door, he thought that he might possibly be at the back one. So he went round to the back door opened it, and looked out upon the piazza. There on the porch with eyes shining in the sun stood the terrible lion roaring louder than thunder. He looked as if he were orange-colored in the sun, but he wasn't; he was golden for he was Mr. Lion with a great big tawny mane.

Very, very fortunately Mr. Rabbit had the wand which the fairy had given him. He remembered it, and struck Mr. Lion. In an instant the terrible beast with open jaws and big white teeth had vanished: there Mr. Lion stood, but he wasn't Mr. Lion at all, he was a maiden!

She was very beautiful for she had gentle blue eyes, golden curls, and little teeth white as pearls. Her eyes twinkled in the sun, and her curls were iridescent in it. She wore diamonds round her neck, and had on the most beautiful dress that was ever seen: it was pink satin with gold lace about it, the lace was china and in the sun it sparkled like her eyes. She was standing stock-still smiling at Mr. Rabbit.

"Oh Mr. Rabbit," she said in a few minutes, "my step-mother did not like me; she was not kind to me; she did not give me anything to eat, and did not think that I was as beautiful as I am. With a wand she changed me into a lion, and when I was a lion I was afraid until you changed me into a maiden once more. I wish to live with you always, and not go back to my ugly stepmother."

Then Mr. Rabbit piped up and said in a shrill voice: "I have people to play with, a brother and a sister, and their names are Mrs. Spinning-Wheel and Mr. Horse. You may come and live with us, too."

The maiden smiled and ran toward Mr. Rabbit as fast as she could. She hurried past him and through the back door and into the house. Both Mrs. Spinning-Wheel and Mr. Rabbit exclaimed at the beauty of the maiden. Her eyes twinkled no more now for she was not standing in the sun, but she was as beautiful as when she was.

The fragile lace still sparkled a little bit, but not so much as when she was in the sun.

"What's your name?" questioned Mrs. Spinning-Wheel and Mr. Rabbit together.

"Yes, what is your name?" asked Mr. Rabbit alone.

"Miss Silver-Leaf Beauty," replied the maiden.

Mr. Horse was still in Mrs. Spinning-Wheel's bed for he did not think that Mr. Lion was gone. He thought that the lion was still round the house, and he was waiting for Mr. Rabbit to come and tell him when it was safe to get up.

"Come on Mr. Horse!" called Mr. Rabbit, "the lion is gone."

"All right," said he sleepily. "I'll come; but it don't seem possible that the lion should be gone; I don't think anybody could make a lion go away so quick as that. You sure are a smart 'un to drive away a lion so quick. It's not easy to drive away a lion, you know; there's sum'thin that they can always do and it is not easy to drive them away."

Then Mr. Horse forgot all about being sleepy, and sprang up out of bed. He rushed down stairs like a steam engine and clapped his hands for joy when he saw the maiden. "How'd she ever come here"? he asked quickly. "My ain't she beautiful!"

"I touched Mr. Lion with my wand and to protect you I changed him into a maiden. She is coming to live with us always."

"Oh goody!" exclaimed Mr. Horse.

Because Mr. Horse had said "Oh goody" so loud the maiden heard him, and turned her face to him.

"How'd yuh do, and are you well?" said Mr. Horse.

Mr. Horse did not say her name because he did not know it, but the maiden turned to him and said: "good afternoon to you, Mr. Horse, and I am quite well indeed, thank you."

"What's yuh name?" asked Mr. Horse smiling.

Before the maiden had time to answer Mrs. Spinning-Wheel said: "her name is Miss Silver-Leaf Beauty."

"Ain't that a queer name"! said Mr. Horse suddenly.

"Yes, it is a queer name," said Mrs. Spinning-Wheel. Pretty soon she said: "Miss Silver-Leaf—?"

"What do you wish to say to me?" said the maiden.

"Do you know what I am going to give to you?" was Mrs. Spinning-Wheel's next question to the maiden.

"No," said the maiden in a voice that sounded like the wind stirring through some pine needles.

"You stay there, Silver-Leaf, and I'll get you a hundred of them," continued Mrs. Spinning-Wheel.

So the maiden stayed there being entertained by the other people, and Mrs. Spinning-Wheel took out of a little box in another room a hundred rings with rubies in them.

When she was standing at the door of the room, she said: "close your eyes, Silver-Leaf, and do not open them till I say 'ready'."

The maiden closed her eyes, and Mrs. Spinning-Wheel went into the room where they were. She had the box which she had taken the rings out of, and she put the rings back into it.

Still Silver-Leaf had her eyes closed.

Mrs. Spinning-Wheel took a bit of paper, a pencil, and a strong orange-colored string; in the paper she wrapped up the bundle of rings, tied it with the string, and wrote on it "From Mrs. Spinning-Wheel,—Miss Silver-Leaf Beauty". She had the rings done up in cotton so that they would not get broken in the box, by rattling about. She handed Miss Silver-Leaf the precious package.

She took it, untied the bow that the orange string was tied in, took off the paper and the cover of the box. Then she was very much surprised to see that the things, whatever they were, were wrapped in cotton; so they were very precious. Very, very slowly she unwrapped one corner of the cotton and saw one ruby shining; and when she had unwrapped another bit of cotton she saw some gold, and that was the ring, for all the rings that the family owned were made of gold. Then she undid the next bit of cotton a little faster, and the rest of it she undid very fast. And my! was'nt she surprised when she saw those rings! Then she counted them, and saw that Mrs. Spinning-Wheel hadn't missed one, but had given her a hundred, just as she said that she would.

"Thank you for the rings" said the maiden; "they are certainly very pretty."

"You are certainly quite welcome" replied Mrs. Spinning-Wheel. "But I think it's about time we went to bed now."

[14]

"All right" said Mr. Rabbit; "I'm willing."

So they all had their supper and went upstairs. Then Miss Silver-Leaf took off her beautiful pink satin dress with the gold china lace and went to bed in the guest-room. Then Mrs. Spinning-Wheel and Mr. Rabbit got into Mrs. Spinning-Wheel's bed; and Mr. Horse slept in another room. That's what he did. And they all were soon fast asleep.

Chapter IV

The next morning when they were all wide awake, (except Miss Silver-Leaf who was very tired because, you see, when she had been a lion she had been wandering about trying to catch the family for dinner), Mrs. Spinning-Wheel, Mr. Horse, and Mr. Rabbit saw the sun neither high nor low in the sky. The rain was falling, not in a few little drops that pattered against the windowpane but in torrents. It just poured! They all were suddenly blinded by a big flash of lightning, and then they were all startled by the boom, boom, boom of the thunder; the yellow lightning streaked the sky like fire while the thunder sounded like a great big angry bear up in the heavens. It rattled the windows, too; and the lightning stripped the bark off the trees; in a minute there was a big flash of lightning that covered every window in the house and then there was a heavy clap of thunder that awoke Miss Silver-Leaf Beauty; this clap of thunder sounded right out in the family's garden. No wonder it had wakened the maiden! They all nearly cried when they thought that the storm was going to last a long time, but as they watched the sky seemed brighter and in a minute the sun came out making the most beautiful rainbow in the sky. The colors in it were green, purple, indigo, red, lighter purple that is called blue, yellow, and darker yellow that is called orange.

As they watched, the rainbow seemed to fade away: first, the green disappeared, then the purple, then the indigo, then the red, then the blue, then the yellow, and finally, the last of the orange faded out. Then Mrs. Spinning-Wheel said: "I think I will go out and get some eggs for breakfast". They all agreed, and so she did.

When she came back she had a dozen of eggs. Then they went down stairs and set the table for breakfast. They got a large dish and in it put the twelve eggs. Mrs. Spinning-Wheel sat down at her place, Mr. Horse sat down at his, and Mr. Rabbit sat down in his chair. First, Mrs. Spinning-Whell cracked an egg, and, lo and behold!, instead of being all yellow and white as most eggs are, it had a baby spinning-wheel in it! How surprised she was! Then Mr. Rabbit cracked an egg and, lo and behold!, instead of being all yellow and white as most eggs are, it had a baby rabbit in it! How surprised he was! Then Mr. Horse cracked an egg and, lo and behold!, instead of being all yellow and white as most eggs are, it had a baby horse in it. Then each cracked another egg to eat instead of eating up their babies. Only those three had babies in them, so after the family had eaten one egg each, there were still five eggs left over for the next day.

The babies didn't last long; they each fell sick and died.

I think I will end my story here. Mr. Horse remained white the rest of his life to the great joy of all the others; Mr. Rabbit kept the fairy wand, and so if any wild beast came he could touch him with the wand and change him into something that wouldn't eat them up; the maiden kept the ruby-stoned rings; Mr. Horse went on with his bad grammar day after day; and Mrs. Spinning-Wheel was happy, too. They were all happy all the rest of their lives.

And that is the end of the story, O best beloved.

This is an unusually competent piece of writing for a six-year-old, but it reflects interests and ways of thinking which are not at all unusual for that age. Perhaps it will not spoil the story to add a few comments.

As Barbara's mother and father knew, she was a little disappointed with the color of the rocking-horse she got on her fifth birthday. It may be that this disappointment furnished a starting-point for her magical fantasy. Let us notice, however, that the horse in the story has traits besides a dark color which are somewhat undesirable. He talks bad grammar, he is unruly and a bit violent, and at the same time a bit of a coward and lazy. It is Mrs. Spinning-Wheel who wishes for his improvement in color, who tries to ride him and is thrown, and into whose bed he creeps when danger threatens. It is Mr. Rabbit, however, who with the aid of the fairy and the fairy's wand actually changes his color, makes Mrs. Spinning-Wheel sound again after she has been thrown, and protects both him and Mrs. Spinning-Wheel from the menacing lion. Mr. Rabbit, we know, has his counterpart in Barbara's life in the toy bunny repaired by Mr. Oberg, the bunny to whom she apparently addressed the lines of verse quoted earlier. It is too much to suppose that the Mr. Rabbit of the story is Barbara's special representative, her alter ego? He is at least the central character. By the same line of reasoning we should be led to connect Mrs. Spinning-Wheel with Barbara's mother, and Mr. Rocking-Horse with her father. Perhaps this is to inquire too curiously. All it does for us, at the most, is to help embed the story in Barbara's family history, and to suggest what some of her own feelings were—not at all what the "real" external circumstances were. Without going beyond the story itself and making these questionable identifications, we can see that Barbara has represented a set of personal relations in which there is a correct and generous person (Mrs. Spinning-Wheel), a very interesting but somewhat ungoverned person (Mr. Horse), and a brave, active, magical person (Mr. Rabbit) who tries to do good things.

Now, the world in which these persons live is charged with beauty and magic. Jewels, flowers, a butterfly-fairy, a storm and a rainbow, are some of the furnishings. In this world two quite extraordinary events occur: a ferocious lion is changed into a beautiful, gentle maiden; and three breakfast eggs are found to contain infantile replicas of those who break them. The incident of the eggs reveals that Barbara had some understanding of the mystery of reproduction—combined with that realization of the shadow of death which hangs over her earlier writings. Do children of five or six or younger brood over birth and death? Of course they do. Barbara is no exception.

And the lion? What are we to make of him? He is an impressive figure. His roar at a distance scares the fairy, in spite of her magical powers; it also scares Mr. Horse and Mrs. Spinning-Wheel. Only brave Mr. Rabbit dares to confront him, opening first this door and then that to come at him. And when at last he is seen, the vision is no anticlimax to the roar. He is magnificent. *"There on the porch with eyes shining in the sun stood the terrible lion roaring louder than thunder.*" He has the grandeur, the brilliance, and the blazing color of the sun, and his voice is that of the stormy sky; and he is indeed terrible, not only in power but in intention too, for he comes to eat them all. One is reminded of I Peter 5:8, "your adversary the devil, as a roaring lion, walketh about, seeking whom he may devour." But hidden within this terror is a most lovely lady, all gentleness and grace, waiting for the stroke of Mr. Rabbit's wand to appear. This is Beauty herself, always present even in the most threatening and destructive aspects of nature: the rainbow after the storm of the next chapter, the honeycomb in the lion's carcass of which Samson made a riddle, the life-giving waters that Moses made to spring out of the desert rock with his magic rod. Barbara's Mr. Lion sounds like the most fundamental of archetypes.

It would be interesting to know if at this time Barbara herself exhibited any of the ferocity of a lion. Other children who make up such stories (and they are common) may do so. Such was the case with a little boy of four-and-a-half, whose father allows me to use the following notes taken unedited from a sporadic diary. For some period of time this boy was preoccupied with various imaginary animals, some good (he called them his "friends"), and some bad; and occasionally he would himself assume one of the animal roles and play it out vigorously. His stories sometimes involved strong language, to match the violence of the action and the very ugly character of certain "bad lions." At four-and-a-half a child may, given freedom of expression, be less decorous than at six. One diary entry is this:

> After his afternoon nap period (he did not sleep), he told me another story about the "wild lion." This bad lion, that roars dreadfully and is as large as the whole world, descended on his animal "friends" to devour them. But the good lion stuck his claws into him, the cow gored him, the chipmunk came with a little knife and cut his legs off, the goose cut off his head, the pony cut off his "front part" (indicating his abdomen), and others cut off his tail: so

"dog" and "pussy" were saved from being eaten. The dis-
membered beast was then gathered up and eaten by the
victors.—Then he began telling me about a much worse
lion—one which wanted to "do-do" all over everyone. The
band of friends destroyed this one also, poking out his eyes
and cutting off his "do-do bottom."—In the evening before
supper, at my request, he drew the bad lion: the head on
one sheet, the body on another; and also heads of "dog,"
"pussy," "good lion," "cow," and "chipmunk." The facial
expressions of all these, which were drawn on a single sheet,
were uniformly pleasant, and the faces, with minor differences, looked alike. The face of the bad lion wore a fierce
expression; and to emphasize his "wildness" further, scrib-
bled lines were drawn erratically and vigorously over the
whole sheet.

Two days later, the diary contains this entry:

Again two stories: (1) a bad man driving a tar-truck is
going to try to run over Dog, Pussy, Chipmunk, and friends;
but they are going to shoot him, throw rocks at him, and
flatten him out flatter than a leaf; and then they're going to
run the tar-truck over him. (2) A bad wild lion is going to
attack them and try to eat them up. This lion has a mouth
as big as the whole world, and eats sand and rocks and all
the big people. Its wee-weer also is big as the world; and
the wee-weer is made of do-do, and the do-do place is made
of wee-wee; and the wee-weer which is made of do-do is lo-
cated on top of its head, and it eats its own do-do and wee-
wee and spits do-do into the mouths of all the people, and it
eats up its own legs and spits them out back on to its body.
After describing the horrible monster and leaping up and
down with excitement, he began defending me from it by
ear-splitting yells and sudden rushes, beating it back from
the window with a book; for it seems it was trying to get in
to eat me.

This boy's bad lion has a much uglier look than Barbara's, and his method of dealing with it (attack) is different from hers (magical transformation); but it seems basically the same kind of monster: it has enormous power, and it threatens to devour all in its path. In the boy's case, there is some kind of relationship between his own aggressive behavior around the house, especially as directed toward his mother and father, and the dreadful acts of this bad lion, this malevolent adversary of cosmic proportions. To a certain extent he *is* the bad lion, though at the same time he is, along with his "friends," the lion's opponent. In Barbara's story, the magical transformation of the lion into a charming maiden may perhaps indicate a similar identification. Even a little girl is not always "sugar and spice and everything nice."

But we surely have not said everything when we note a possible connection between a child's aggressive feelings and a tremendous spiritual lion which expresses them on a grand scale. The lion is not simply a child's aggression, magnified and projected into imaginary space. It is the terrible power of the universe, the power of thunderstorms and blazing suns, the power of earthquakes and tornadoes, coming straight at the child and his loved ones with the sun in his eyes or the darkness of night in his eyes, to overwhelm them and annihilate them. How courageous the little boy and the little girl are, and how resourceful! Grandeur to match the lion's is in their tiny human bodies. Particularly blest was Barbara that she could find the lovely maiden inside the universal carnivore.

Chapter II

One cannot impose a simple pattern on the varied and shifting interests of a child. Yet there are temporary anchoring points: members of the family, special friends, and living and non-living playthings. Mr. Oberg continued for a long time to be Barbara's chief correspondent; he was also a source of marvellous gifts, and he received the full warmth of her love. In March, 1920, she recounts in a letter the arrival of *"the BEAUTIFULLEST yellow chair in the world,"* one of his gifts; but adds, *"There was one thing that was missing: it was you, YOURSELF."* On April 26, 1920, a handwritten letter to him runs:

My dear Mr. Oberg:
Thank you very, very, very much for the little card with the picture of the three rabbits on it, and the little song that you made up for it.
Now that the snow has all melted and the skiis and snowshoes are put away, I am climbing trees and bushes, digging holes with sticks, picking ferns and other things such as maple blossoms, and that is about all.
Love from the little girl to the little boy.

Barbara

One must feel the emphasis of that third "very," and smell the fresh air outdoors where the little girl climbs and digs holes and picks ferns and maple blossoms, to appreciate the full energy of this declaration. But Mr. Oberg is not the sole recipient of her love. On May 7, 1920, she writes to her grandmother (I retain her spelling):

Dear Ding:
Thank you very much for the little May baskets; they are lovely, and I'm going to put flowers in them.

I'm now going to tell you something that will make you very happy: The blueets are in blossom, and the violets and the dandylions are beginning to blossom.

The butterflies are comming fast now. Sometimes I sit down in a chair and suddenly I see a white Butterfly fly in circles about the potato patch; and I jump from my seat and run after it and see it alight and I tiptoe up to it, and I am just about to open my fingers to take it by the wing when away it would fly.

I miss you terribly. I hope you will be back before the buttercups come because I want you to see every one of them.

The love overflows in every direction, disregarding the boundaries between living and non-living, human and non-human. Members of the family are referred to under animal names—Mother-Cat, Fox, Daddy-Dog—and stuffed toy animals are treated as one's own kindred. Thus a letter of June 23, 1920, addressed to a person both fictional and real, introduces a "sister" whom we encounter in other contexts where the unwarned reader might be startled into the mistaken conclusion that Barbara had ceased to be an only child, as when she renders *"nonillion thanks"* to Mr. Oberg in November for a collection of beads and shells and states that she has made two necklaces, *"one for Little Sister, and one for me."* But in the June letter to *"Dear Fox,"* there is no obscurity: *"You should come and see my new animals. One of them is a little brown squirrel with a strip of white running down his front."*—Here there is a critical turning-point, a change of sex.—*"Her head turns, her arms turn, her tail turns, and her feet turn. Her real name is Frisk Squirrel, but she is Grandfather Bunny's little sister and so I call her Little Sister."*

In affectionate relationships it is not enough to have feelings and express them. One must act, and act for the benefit of the beloved. When Barbara makes a necklace for herself from Mr. Oberg's shells and beads she demonstrates their value for her, she thanks him in the profoundest sense; and the adornment is as much for him as for herself. Children are often accused of a narrow self-interest, in taking things so willingly from others or in calling attention to their activities so insistently. But what better way is

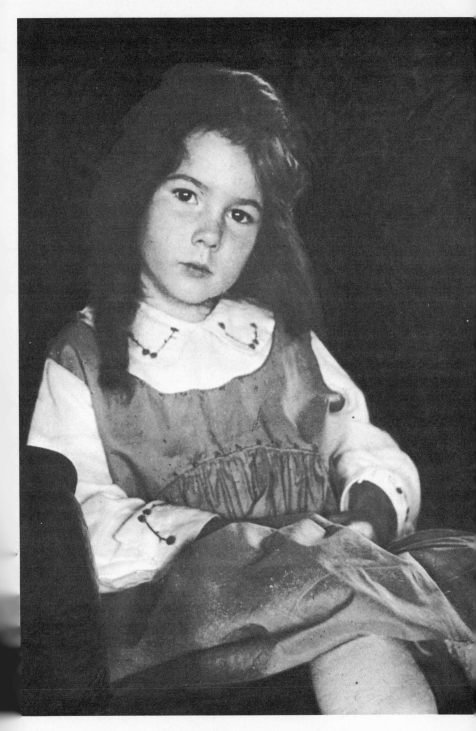

Mr. Oberg's portrait of Barbara at about six

there of expressing love than by sharing one's delight in oneself, and one's activities, with the giver and admirer? So Barbara writes to Mr. Oberg late in 1920, *"I wish you would come down to see me walk and run on snow-shoes because I can walk and run on them,"* and, on another occasion, *"I have learned to ice-skate, and I hope the next time you come to see me, you will see me skate in the Arena."* How energetically she looks out of the picture which Mr. Oberg took of her early in 1920, demanding attention, yes, but reciprocally giving her own. Again and again she mingles with her thanks for some favor a regret that he was not present to share some experience with her or issues an invitation to visit her. A letter of March 30, 1921, tempts him with flowers and a story:

My dear Mr. Oberg:

As you wanted me to tell you the flowers are coming very fast; and now I suppose the wild flowers will begin to come. But I don't think we shall find many buttercups and daisies because they like the open places, and we have the woods,—but still we may find a few in the fields across the road. I think we shall find some violets, and the wood flowers will be very thick. The crocuses and snow-drops have even gone by. The yellow forsythia is on it's way out, just as the little brook is on it's way to join the big river.

You have read the Spinning-Wheel, the Rocking-Horse, and the Rabbit, haven't you? Well, I am beginning a new adventure of how they go traveling to China. If you will come to see me I will read it to you.

Two months later (May 26, 1921) she is urging him to come and stay the whole summer, giving details of the flower schedule:

If you want a rest from the city you come down here because this is just like the country. We live near the city but there are so many trees around our house that any one who came to visit this house would not know whether this is the country or city. I wish you could have been here when the purple violets came, but still we have the white and yellow violets to watch for. If you want to be here when the buttercups are in bloom you will have to hurry up and come because their petals are dropping fast. I think you will be here when the daisies come because yesterday I found the first one. I also think you will be here when the white and yellow violets begin to dot the grass. You certainly will have to hurry if you want to see the last few wild geraniums; you will have to come this week Saturday, and maybe they will all be gone by that time. The pink and white clover are here, but I don't think I can find any more blue-eyed grass. I'll tell you why,—the only place I know to get blue eyed grass is over on the University land, and they are cutting down the grass over there. I also found a queer little flower that looked like an aster. It was purplish-white with a pretty little yellow centre, and ever so many stamens and petals; when you pick it it lasts a long time if you will only give it fresh water every day. I'm sure you can see the iris if you only come soon enough because there's only one blue one out now. The azaleas I'm afraid you have missed; but the rhododendrons are magnificent, and if you'll only come in time you will see them. I've told you all about these flowers so that you will want to come and see me.

Barbara at this period was keeping a flower diary, in which she recorded minute details of their color and structure. At a slightly later time she began a butterfly diary. Like other scientific cataloguings these accounts grow tedious, and one admires the patient accuracy of the little naturalist who submits herself to such discipline. After enumerating the spots and lines of color of one butterfly *"almost too beautiful to describe,"* she almost audibly rebels against the impossible task with: *"Now I guess it would be best to let the little fairy go because I have kept him about a half an hour to describe him, and you know they can't live forever. So we shall let him spend the rest of his life among the flowers and the trees, instead of in an old sive."* Fortunately, she has left us descriptions of action, too, as well as of color and form, as in this passage about her kitten, Buff (in a letter to her Cousin Helen, July 6, 1921):

I'll tell you now something about what Buff does. She will sit in my lap and purr and purr until it seems as if she would purr her throat weak. Then she looks so cunning when she is sitting up and washing her face with one paw, and she will wash my own face with one little pink tongue. *Her tongue is so rough that it seemed to tear the skin off my face as I was writing your letter this morning. If you drag a string in front of her she will run after it with great force; I suppose she runs after it so fast because she is anxious to get hold of it. Also, when I trow A cork or a piece of paper to her she will run to it, clasp it in her front paws, jump up in the air with it, twist half her body 'round while she is up, and come down with her eyes wide open. While she is doing this, her ears are turned forward as far as they will go, and her eyes are as far open as they can be.*

The kitten is no more active than herself. During the summer of 1921, at *"a certain beach called Indian Neck,"* she writes to Mr. Oberg: *"I have learned to swim the Dog Paddle. Once the tide was low enough for me to go out to the raft. I went out and jumped off and I bounced on the sand the way a tennis ball would bounce on the sidewalk."* In August the beach is exchanged for camping under a tent with Father and Mother, sleeping *"on three folding cots which are even more comfortable than Cousin Hattie's beach beds which I slept on once."* At the same time, there is always and everywhere literature. She intends to take along on her camping excursion a story about an eagle translated from the Swedish by her old friend, a story in which a princess is rescued from a giant—so delightful that Barbara wants *"to take it away with me to read to the children, and to myself."* She wants to share everything:

Over the hills for
   columbine,
The flower is red
It is yours; it is mine
The sweet
   columbine.

In November, as she tells Mr. Oberg in a letter which she pretends to be telephoning, she dances The Seven Jumps and The Crested Hen in bright little Swedish costumes at the Westville club-house, *"the first time I ever danced before so big an audience."* This letter is signed, *"With love from Barbara Newhall Follett to her most loving friend Mr. Oberg."*

If Barbara lacked anything, it was other children. She was far more acquainted with adults. Yet it cannot be said that she felt the lack or tried to supply it through her imagination. Her "pretend" friends were not children. She tells Mr. Oberg about some of her imaginary companions in a letter of January 12, 1922:

I pretend that Beethoven, the Two Strausses, Wagner, and the rest of the composers are still living, and they go skating with me, and when I invite them to dinner, a place has to be set for them; and when I have so many that the table won't hold them all, I make my family sit on one side of their chair to make room for them. My abreviation for the Two Strausses is the Two S's. Beethoven, Wagner, and the Two S's have maids; Beethoven's maid's name is Katherine Velvet, Wagner's maid's name is Katherine Loureena (she got the name Loureena when she was a little bit of a girl because she loved to skate in the Arena), and Strauss's maid's name is Sexo Crimanz. . . . Now I am going to tell you about a funny accident that Wagner had. One morning when I had two chairs set out, one for Beethoven and the other for Wagner, I hadn't pretended long enough to get my family used to them, and Daddy suddenly grabbed the chair that Wagner was sitting in, but I held on to it squealing: "Hey, that's Wagner's chair!" Then he went around to Beethoven, and I was looking suspiciously at him all the time. But he turned around again and didn't bother Beethoven. I suppose that when he got around there, he thought that Beethoven was there.

These companions are connected, as easily inferred, with the practice of music, which moved from percussion to piccolo and, later, violin. In a poem of January 15, 1922, she tells something about her musical experience:

When I go to orchestra rehearsals,
    there are often several passages for the
    Triangle and Tambourine
        together.
When they are together,
    they sound like a big piece of metal
    that has broken in thousandths
        and is falling to the ground.

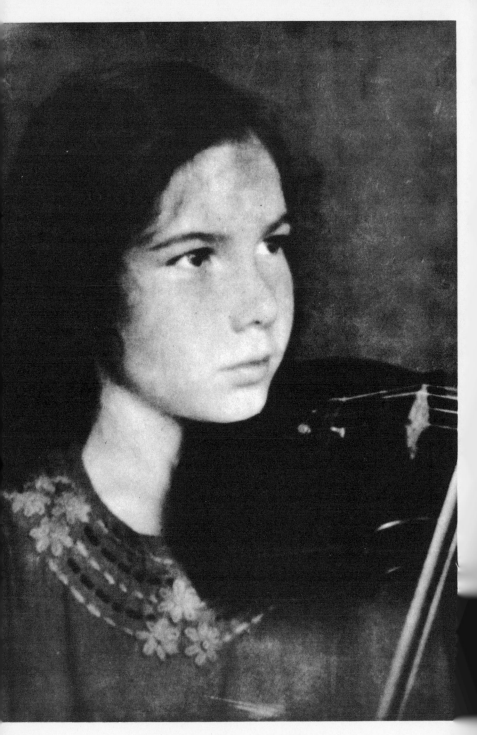

Barbara at eight with violin

On the same day she wrote a poem about visual experience:

When I look into my kaleidoscope,
The world I see
Is the Colored World.
Inside
Is a forest
With flowers scattered all over the ground,
And glass trees in it;
And when I look 'way off into it,
The colors seem to run together,
Forming a brown mountain
Far, far away.
Once,
When I looked into it,
There was a six-pointed star
Around every other tree.

She herself at times glitters and glows like the colored world of the kaleidoscope. To Mr. Oberg she writes, January 12: "*Saturday I had a show, and I wish you could have been here to see it. It was a dance, and I danced in tinsel costumes. . . . For one costume, I had on a white dress, a tinsel band around my forehead, a band of tinsel around the bottom of my dress, a little circle of tinsel hanging every little way, from the band of tinsel around the bottom of my dress, a tinsel belt, a band of tinsel around my cuffs, and a band of tinsel sewed around the neck of my dress. . . . For the second costume I had on another white dress. The costume was: a pink ribbon for a belt, and sewed on to the right hand side of my belt was a pink artificial rose; around my forehead was the same band of tinsel, as in the first costume and in my hair were some more artificial flowers. I gave six dances—two dances in each costume. The third costume was the one described in the other letter. I will now describe Peggy's dance. She gave one dance, and that one came after mine. I had on in that dance a little yellow dress made out of material that shows all your underclothes, and by mistake the flowers stayed in my hair.*" Poor Peggy! We don't know what costume *she* wore or whether she danced ill or well.

Fairies occupied an important place in Barbara's life from an early date. For her, there was no strict boundary between the fairy world and the everyday world. After all, most of the elements of the fairy world are found on this side of the boundary. Barbara tells a correspondent in a letter of February 28, 1922, that she has been entranced by *The Treasure of the Isle of Mist,* particularly the chapter entitled "Fiona in the Fairy-World," from which she quotes with satisfaction a description of the *"fair country of green grass and temperate airs"* where the heroine is confronted with a choice between two paths, a broad pleasant one passing under lemon trees and a narrow rocky one ascending a bare hillside; urged on toward the easy, pleasant way by invisible spirits who wish to do her harm, the story heroine is almost stepping into the rocky path in opposition to them when the magic feather in her hand turns and reveals to her that, for once, her spiritual opponents have been trying to deceive her by openly driving her into the true path—i.e., the one bordered by anemones under the lemon trees. Barbara reacts by writing stories of her own: "The Treasure of the Isle of Mist *has got me so interested in treasure that I also wrote a book about treasure, called* The Adventures of Curis. *It was also about a little girl that went hunting treasures, as you may find out when I make a good copy of the story and send it to you, and I hope you will like it. As soon as I had finished that story, I began another one called* The Magic Violin. *This I wrote because I got so extremely interested in the violin that I got for my birthday. If you like* Curis, *I will send you* The Magic Violin; *and if you like that I will send you the next story,* The Allegro of the Earth, *which is about a little kitten that was so happy and gay and bouncy all the time that people called her the Allegro of the Earth."*

At first sight the fairy world is just like the ordinary world, though perhaps more varied and more brilliant; but then one begins to notice differences in the population and the language. In the following letter to a Miss Deane who had sent her some trailing arbutus, Barbara moves from the lovely realities of this everyday earth to the similar but altered realities of fairyland:

The eighth of May I may go off with Daddy into the woods to find and pick some trailing arbutus. We mean to find two little glades, one with ever-green trees around it, with the needles scattered over moss, and the other full of flowers where we can pick all we want to: we are going to have luncheon in the woods and have a whole day to ourselves. The year before last we went into the woods together, and for the first time I saw some yellow adder's-tongue and also some anemones. When I saw the yellow adder's-tongue I didn't know what it was at first, but after a while I told Daddy that I had once seen in the wildflower book a picture of a flower that looked something like that one, and that they called it yellow adder's-tongue. Every one that we found had two narrow pointed leaves near the bottom and a long smooth stem; we pulled the flower right above the leaves and the stem slipped out from between them, so that no leaves were picked with the flower.

We have had for flowers squills, violets, bluets, and daffodils, and the crocuses and snowdrops have gone long ago. For birds we have had crows, blackbirds, I think some starlings, bluejays, and we have seen one flicker; we have also seen some little gray birds that we couldn't see well enough to know what they were. Some of the birds that I have named stay all winter, but I haven't seen any birds all winter.

Yesterday I started writing a fairy play. There are three fairies in it, Viren, Raindu, and Rondaintu, and they all have very important parts. The play is called The Fairy's Nest, because the fairies all make a little nest on a big rock covered with vines. There is also a goblin in the play, who is the worst enemy of the fairies. The fairy parts are written in poetry, but the goblin part isn't. It may have four acts, or the third and the fourth may be put together; I'm sure I don't know. It may even turn out to be a one-act play.

I have also written a bird book that has got in it eighteen imaginary birds, with a description of their songs, calls, nests, and eggs. It really is very interesting, but the most interesting birds are the fisheens and the finourios. I am going to have a book published full of my stories, and some of my birds will be put in it, and then you can read about them and their wonderful habits and ideas.

The above letter was written May 2, 1922. In one of May 22 to Mr. Oberg we learn more about the fisheens and finourios: *"The finourios are all very pretty, but the knowraino finourio has the power to change his coat and also his song before it rains. The fisheens, also, are quite pretty, and they are the birds that sit on rocks sticking out of the water, and catch the fish as they come by. But the short-billed fisheen has to duck his head under water to catch the fish. The total length of the fresh-water fisheen's bill is six inches; the total length of the salt-water fisheen's bill is four inches; the total length of the short-billed fisheen's bill is one and a half inches; and the total length of the silvery fisheen's bill is four and two eighths inches."*

In the references to the fisheens and finourios and the names of the fairies there is a hint of a new development: the invention of a private language called Farksoo—the language of the inhabitants of Farksolia, a land on a planet twice the size of ours and far away from here. A letter of thanks to Mrs. Lathrop for a book by De la Mare which Mrs. Lathrop had illustrated contains more information about the language (the letter is dated May 12, 1922):

Thank you ever and ever so much for sending me a copy of Walter de la Mare's Down A-Down Derry. I think the pictures are wonderful and especially the frontispiece is a wonderful illustration of a fairy. I also love the poem that goes with that picture. I think it is perfectly wonderful the whole business.

I have now started a story about kittens, and the most important character is Verbiny the princess who found the mother-cat in the woods, caught her, and tamed her. One of the four kittens had a black back arched up like a kangaroo rat's, and at the top of each white stocking was a band of yellow. All the kittens catch little crickets and grasshoppers, and one of the kittens catches a bay mouse, and a kitten named Citrolane catchs two sparrows, one with each paw. But just a little while after the kittens are born they want so much to see what is on the other side of the fence that fences in their property that they climb up over it and jump down and almost land on a porcupine, but he good-naturedly steps aside in time. In a chapter called Springtime I have written down a little poem in a secret language that Verbiny called Farksoo. In the secret language it was this:

Painting by I. Pulis Lathrop of Barbara at Lake Sunapee in the summer of 1922

Ar peen maiburs barge craik coo
Peen yar fis farled cray pern.
Peen darndeon flar fooloos lart ain birdream.
Avee lart ain caireen ien tu cresteen der tuee,
Darnceen craik peen bune.
I will now translate it as best as I can.
As the (and maiburs means a flower that comes in
May,) begin to come the air is filled with perfume,
the dandelion fluff floats like a, (and birdream
means something very beautiful.)
Also like a fairy in her dress of gold,
Dancing to the wind.

A portrait done by I. Pulis Lathrop, the mother of the correspondent to whom the above letter was addressed, shows Barbara as she was a few weeks later at Sunapee, the vacation spot where she and her family went summer after summer. Here at Sunapee, though no doubt she thought about the fairies and Farksolia a great deal, she was vividly in touch with all the world around her. The quality and intensity of that relationship can be caught in letters written from Sunapee to her father. For example:

The Cottage in the Woods
August 8, 1922

Dear Daddy:

If you had only waited till today to go home you would not have missed a wonderful sight. Late in the afternoon I went out for a little row in the boat. It began to sprinkle and so I came back. A few moments after I had reached the house the sprinkling changed to pelting, and a storm arose over the lake. I certainly think that some other people got it worse than we did. The wind blew the rain and part of the surface of the lake eastward, sometimes blowing them a foot or so above the water, and sometimes rolling them on the water. The wind did not let the rain fall where it wanted to, but blew it along a few feet beyond the spot. It was certainly wonderful to watch!

You know that I have put the baby lizard in the minnow pail. Of course there was no other place to put the tadpoles but in the lake. So I left the tin in the water by the boat tied to one of the oar-locks, and I kept thinking that they weren't safe and worrying about them part of the night. In the morning I came down to see how they were and the tin was on its side and the cover was slit open, but —there was not a tadpole there. But I don't care much for I know that they are safe and sound in Little Sunapee Lake. And besides I think that they will live better.

The baby lizard is so little that I have some trouble to find him when I want him, but I am sure he is all right, in that great pail. The hurt lizard hasn't died yet and I think he will be all right sooner or later. I hope so don't you?

Love and kisses from Barbara

to

Dear Daddy-Dog.

It was during this summer at Sunapee that Barbara acquired an important new correspondent. Mr. St. John, Dean of the Theological Seminary at Auburn, N. Y., was camping alone in a road cutout at the head of the lane that led to the Follett cottage, and Barbara and he were drawn together by their common interest in all aspects of Nature. After she returned home and received a letter from him, she wrote him a full account of her summer:

October 22, 1922
708 Orange Street
New Haven, Connecticut

Dear Mr. St. John:

I was very much pleased to get a letter from you so soon, but I am very sorry that I haven't answered it any sooner than this. The shell which you sent to me I thought was very beautiful, and when it is held up to the light there are many curving and twisting streaks in it that can't be seen otherwise.

Up at Sunapee I had two adventures with red squirrels that I think you would like to hear about, since you are so much interested in the wild folk. The first one happened this way. I was playing in the woods, and I heard a lot of red squirrels chattering together. I walked toward the sound, until I came to a little clearing, carpeted with the leaves of the clintonia, the berries gone, and there I sat down to watch. I kept so still that before long a red squirrel came out of the underbrush and peered at me. Then with a frightened shriek he scurried away. He only went as far as a tree five or six feet back into the woods. Then he turned around and came back to peer at me again. Then with another shriek he went back to the tree. It was mere curiosity. He came, peered, and went, five or six times, with a little shriek each time he went, until finally with a bound he scurried away perhaps to tell the other squirrels the news. Then, before many minutes had passed, another smaller red squirrel came galloping across the clearing with a nut in his mouth. On the right of where I was sitting was a mound of earth with a couple of trees growing on it, and the red squirrel went behind the two trees, came around, peered at me for a minute, and went into a small hole that I hadn't noticed before, and after he had deposited the nut, came out from another one, as the clearing was near some beech-trees. In this way seven or eight nuts were put in the hole before I went home.

The second adventure happened this way. Before we went home the stretch of beach that goes around to the other little beach where I caught the minnows, was there to go around on, for the water had gone down and left it. One day as I was coming home from the minnow beach that way, I heard a rustle in the woods, and I kept very still because I wanted to understand whatever it meant. Pretty soon a red squirrel came out of the woods in back of the beach, peered at me for a second or two, went back into the woods, and came out again farther down the beach. Then he went down to the water and took a drink. His little pink tongue lapped the water much the way a cat's tongue does. Have you ever seen a red squirrel do that? I presume you have, but Daddy said he never had.

And now I will tell you about something else. I have found many varieties of aquatic plants, most of them very beautiful. I found two especially beautiful ones, one with eight or nine narrow leaves pointed at the top, about two and a half inches long, dark green at the top, and orange coloured at the roots; and the other was a long slender grass, with little brown buds on it, one having a white blossom so small that it could just be seen.

And now for the salamanders. I had been trying desperately to keep them in deep pails, but I never succeeded because they climbed right out. So finally I said to Daddy: "Can you tell me how to keep those lizards in and happy?" And he got a wooden box, asked me to make a garden of mosses and ferns in it, and then he nailed some wire netting over the top of it, cut a rectangular hole in it, and put the lizards in. Once Daddy went up Burpee Hill to get the car, and he brought back to me a lizard about an inch and a quarter long, under the seat. I put it in a dish with some moss in it while I went to ride, and when I came back he was gone. For this was before Daddy had made the cage. Another time before we had fixed the box up, I found another one smaller than that, and I kept him longer. Once I took him out and showed him to Daddy who said: "There ain't no such animal." But alas, one day he got out, and I had the box he was in on the piazza. I'm glad that I didn't have the other baby on the piazza, which is really the most treacherous place for a lizard because it is full of cracks and crevices. But happily I found a lizard smaller than the last, and had the box to put him in. I saw him every day with a lot of other salamanders, and when I left the box out in the rain some nights they would all be out from under the moss the next morning. When we went home I let the lizards go, and I took them out one by one to find the little one, but, though I found some pretty small ones, I didn't find the tiny one. I have a strong suspicion, however, that he had grown to be one of these.

I am sending you a bit of prose about October in Sunapee, for you weren't there to see how beautiful it was.

The bit of Prose, with its title in spaced capital letters, reminds us that there is another dimension to Nature than those which customarily set the boundaries to mortal vision:

OCTOBER

In the radiant sunshine of October the trees on Lake Sunapee are crimson, gold, and red. The reflection of them in the lake is nearly as clear as the trees themselves. Canoeing to one of the crimson shores will mean paddling in painted water, vivid and quivering. One can think of water flowers growing in the painted water and turning red. Only the evergreens stay green, and there on a point of evergreens bordered with crimson maples dance the nymphs night and day, in dresses of red and green. They are gay little fairies, dancing and flying, whispering and talking to one another, in voices clear as bells, catching butterflies and talking to them, and singing with the birds, and having concerts with them. O then life is of happiness and freedom, until one day the radiant leaves fall, and winter draws near.

Chapter III

Absorbed though Barbara was in the study of nature, delighted though she was with sheer physical activity, and surrounded though she was by loving parents and numerous friends, a restlessness drove her beyond the accepted earthly boundaries. She lived much in her imagination, as the careless phrase has it. She even developed her special language, Farksoo, which she attributed to the inhabitants of an extra-terrestrial realm, Farksolia. She built up enough of a Farksoo vocabulary to compose a few brief poems in it, and she was at some pains to outline the history and geography of Farksolia. She was preoccupied with these matters for several years.

An example of Farksoo has already been given (p. 34), a poem whose opening line, *"Ar peen maiburs barge craik coo,"* means in English *"As the mayflowers begin to come."* The Farksoo words are consistently used (for example, "peen" always means "the"), and they were systematically collected into a dictionary, at first on sheets of paper and later (at her father's suggestion) on cards kept in a filing cabinet; but they are constructed on no easily discoverable principles, except that they should look and sound different from their English equivalents. Their main use in Barbara's writings is to provide names for various imaginary plants and animals and for fairies. Yet the Farksoo language, which she herself refers to as "secret," could have been a means of cutting herself off from those who stick to earthly languages. In fact, it was shared with several people, and thus was only in a limited, formal sense a secret language. The same can be said for Farksolia. Potentially, it was a land belonging entirely to herself and the Farksolians. Actually, she shared it with a number of people here on earth.

By early 1923 (when Barbara was eight years, nine months of age) Farksolia had become so much a part of her daily life that she

Barbara at nine or ten in a Farksolian mood

could use it in an offhand fashion in a piece of advice addressed to her mother for the correction of certain faults in her parents and their friends. Perhaps it would not be far from the mark if we took these criticisms as coming from a Farksolian annoyed with the shortcomings of earthlings. A picture of Barbara at age nine or ten standing in the snow and looking haughtily back from the forest cover into which she might at any moment disappear may possibly reflect the right Farksolian mood. Here is the advice, bluntly phrased:

Talk about something! Get rid of your female friends who talk about nothing but their children, and your gentlemen friends who talk about nothing but books and colleges and automobiles. Or, if you can't get rid of them talk about something really worth while. The worst part of this dull talk is that the listeners are interested! Instead of listening intently and gossiping about everybody with your female friend, ——, why don't you say: "I'm not interested can't you talk about anything but other people's affairs?" (I don't mean that you should be really rude, though.) Now think what an effect that would have. You might be able to make your friends real friends instead of pretend friends. Now, why under the sun does Daddy listen so intently when everybody talks about books, books, books with never a moment's rest. Sometimes they do talk a little about automobiles, but these authors are made of books anyhow and they can't talk anything else, even if they tried. Make them! Get it into them that they must talk about something else. You say you have business to do—well, do it! You could get it over in five minutes if you really tried. But you string it out to the last possible detail, as if you really enjoyed it. I can't believe you really do enjoy it, it is so stupid. Now if I were leading a conversation I would first say a good deal about Farksolia, but before my audience got tired of it I would say something about how vile the slaughter of trees is getting. Then I would go back into Farksolia a minute and mention how disgusted a Farksolian would be with this slaughter. Then I would say a little about the gorgeous swallowtail that I saw resting so long amid the green leaves before he flew away. I would ask this one what kind of flower this was, and if she knew anything

[41]

about this variety of bird, and I would say a little about books and poetry. Not that I am putting an abuse on the books. I love books, but this everlasting talk about them all the time (and mostly not interesting ones at that) drives a sensible fellow mad. At least I should think it would.

If you try the plan I have adopted I think you would get many more friends at that. There should be nothing to make a man or a woman happier than a pack of real, honest-to-goodness friends who will always stand by you in your troubles of which you are sure to have many. Make your talk really bright and interesting. Have you ever known—could you ever imagine —— —— to come in saying: "I saw the loveliest butterfly yesterday." or: "I found a marvellously dainty bird's nest as I was coming along to your house."

This page and a half that I have written can be expressed in a very few words: "Make your talk more interesting." Just try this and see if it doesn't work. Of course if it doesn't work, you needn't keep it up but I think it will.

As noted previously, it is from as early as May 12, 1922, when Barbara was just past her eighth birthday, that we have clear indications in a letter that the Farksolian language exists. There it is referred to as "a secret language that Verbiny called Farksoo." Since the language is so closely associated with Verbiny, we may gain some appreciation of Farksolia and its function in Barbara's life by becoming acquainted with Verbiny.

Who is Verbiny? She is a princess, and the heroine of a series of three stories, the first about kittens, the second about butterflies, and the last about birds. In all three stories there is the theme of Verbiny's wish to capture and possess these creatures, and her success in doing so in spite of opposition; and also the theme of their fruitful mating. As a sort of ruler and overseer of animals, and especially of their fertility, she might be a nature goddess; she is at least a princess, with an imperious will. At the same time, she is a little girl, and must work out some kind of tolerable relations with her parents. The situation creates tensions calling for resolution.

In the first of the three stories, Verbiny takes home a cat, Silkris, against the wishes of her mother, who threatens to leave home if Verbiny insists on keeping it. Verbiny defies her mother. Eventually Silkris dies, and Verbiny's mother carries out her threat. Neither event troubles Verbiny. As to the death of Silkris, who is herself a mother: *"That didn't make much difference to the looks of the cat family, for they had Virinits who looked just like her mother."* Furthermore: *"The same day the kitten Silkris had kittens."* In other words, the loss of the original cat mother is adequately compensated for by duplicates of her in a cat who looks like her and in a cat who has the same name and bears new kittens while the first one is dying. Sex is more than a match for death. As to Verbiny's own mother: *"She went away and never came back partly because she hated cats and partly because she thought that Verbiny would spend all her time with them and not do anything else. Don't you believe it she was happy and busy all day with her cats and everything else that a little girl could want."* The opposing mother is thus removed from the scene, and in the subsequent stories there is no further mention of her. In them, the king, Verbiny's father, co-operates fully with her in helping her to capture, keep, and breed butterflies, chipmunks, and birds. There is a strong tie between them. He addresses her as "darling" or "dear," and she openly admires his strength and skill. Nevertheless, there are also moments of conflict: sometimes she says or does things which make him cross at her.

In the Verbiny stories, then, tensions are set up by disagreements or conflicts between the child and her parents. In addition, death enters as a major concern. It enters both as threat and as actuality —as threat in the thought of men hunting the Kangaroo Rat for its fur and in the sight of snakes attempting to kill ducklings; as actuality when Silkris dies, when the kittens kill and devour rats and birds, when the ducklings eat baby snakes, and when the king her father kills the mother snake. We see in Verbiny's reactions to family conflict and death a clue, perhaps, to Barbara's conduct of her affairs in this world. In regard to the mother, we see indifference, or assumed indifference, to her departure. In regard to the father, we see some concern over conflict and even an attempt to apologize to him for being disagreeable. As to death, we see both indifference and protest. And possibly we see a resort to dreaming as an escape from these problems. At any rate, the two dreams which are introduced into the narratives would seem more relevant than they appear on the surface to be if we could take them as reactions to Verbiny's problems, i.e., as attempted escapes into another dimension of life.

Verbiny's dream in the story about the kittens follows a discussion of the danger to the Kangaroo Rat from the men who hunt it for its fur. What follows the dream is the combined tragedy of the death of the mother cat Silkris and the departure of Verbiny's mother. The dream is thus an interlude between the threat of death and its accomplishment, and it takes her from these animal and human concerns into the colorful, flowered and jewelled, though also slightly nonsensical, world of magic. The dream (with slight emendations of spelling and other minor details) runs thus:

That night Verbiny had a lovely dream. She dreamed that she was a long way from home and that she was lost in a beautiful plain. Pretty soon she came to a gate in a fence that had a rose vine trained all over it. "Just like our fence and roses," thought Verbiny. She opened the gate very slowly and cautiously and came right into the garden of Fairy-land. She was amazed! There was a path from the gate right through the garden and on this she walked. On one side of the garden the flowers were arranged the same way as the whole of her own, but on the other side were the trees with flowers on them. There was grass around the flower-beds. The beds where the trees were were circular in shape, instead of rectangular. There were four rows of beds on the left side of the garden: two of the eight front rows were rhododendrons, the next two were fire-blossoms, the next two were low purple lilacs, and the other two were low white lilacs. The second row from the path were four kinds of azaleas two of each kind. There were a queer sort of reddish-pink, red, dark yellow, very light yellow. The next row were fruit-trees two of each kind there were plum-trees, apple-trees, peach-trees, and pear-trees. The last row was all magnolias.

Verbiny walked down the path that went through the middle of the garden. When she came to the end a little fairy stepped out from behind a tree, and touched her with her wand. Instantly she found herself turned into a lovely maiden in a white velvet dress with a white belt covered with precious stones of all kinds. She found herself in a lovely room. All over the ceiling was a vine with precious stones of all kinds in it. Verbiny thought they were fruits, and reached for one of the rubies that had fallen from its grip of the ceiling and was hanging from the vine. Verbiny pulled it down and put it in her mouth. Just then she heard a voice say, "Do not eat it or you will choke."

"Why," asked Verbiny.

"Because it is a ruby. You probably thought it was a strawberry, but it is a ruby," said the Voice.

Verbiny dropped the stone.

"Put it back where it belongs," said the voice.

"Will you tell me how I can put something that has been hanging back again with nothing to do it with."

"Yes."

"How."

"Take something to do it with," said the voice.

"I haven't anything to do it with," said Verbiny, "I said with nothing to do it with."

"I know you said with nothing to do it with," said the voice, "But haven't you got sense enough to take something when there is piles of it right before your eyes."

"Don't treat her that way," begged a new sweet little voice, and a little fairy stepped into the room took up the ruby and placed it on the vine, and went away again.

"Oh I wish all these voices would stop talking to me," sighed Verbiny.

Immediately the room was silent and she lay down on a lovely bed that was in the room and went to sleep. When she woke she found herself sitting up in her own bed.

This dream does succeed in avoiding the death and separation theme of the main story, but it is not altogether rewarding. Rubies mistaken for edible fruit, an impossible task, and annoyingly persistent commanding and quarreling voices are surely a disappointing sequel to the paradisal opulence of the flowery garden at the entrance to fairyland.

Verbiny has another dream in the third story of the series. It follows this unpleasant scene with her father:

> "Child," said the king, "what has come over you? You were never so cross."
>
> "One is always cross when they are sleepy," growled Verbiny in a very cross way, and turning away went up the marble steps to the screened in porch up to the pearl-room, and went to bed.
>
> "I am glad to have you go when you are so cross," muttered the king after her. Verbiny had stopped then, and scowled and went on up.

What does a cross, tired little girl who has just quarreled with her father dream about? The answer in this Verbiny story goes as follows:

> That night Verbiny had a lovely dream. She dreamed that she was walking in the most beautiful flower garden ever seen. The form of a woman flashed before her eyes and vanished. Verbiny shut her eyes and when she opened them she saw a lovely fan floating in the air. It was white with flowers of all colors painted on it. But in another minute she saw that it was not floating but resting on a flight of six golden steps. A voice kept saying: "Up, up, up," very feebly and rising higher at each "up." In a flash Verbiny understood that she was to go up the golden steps, and she went. When she got to the top she found herself in a lovely room with flowers of all colors painted on the floor just as there had been on the fan. The walls and ceiling were covered with painted flowers, too. As the room was fan-shaped Verbiny soon saw that it was the fan that she had seen on the golden steps only with a wall and ceiling, and it was ever so much larger. "I guess that woman I saw was a fairy and changed this fan into a room for me," thought Verbiny. "I must see her again at any rate, she was so lovely."
>
> In a few minutes she went down the steps to the flower garden, where she did not see the woman but an old old woman with white hair and a black dress, trimmed with black lace.

[46]

"Can you tell me," said Verbiny in a trembling voice, "Where the beautiful lady in a dress of many brilliant colors is?" The woman slipped off her black dress and there stood the lady in a pink dress with white lace on it. "What do you want of me?" she asked.

"I wanted to see you you were so lovely," said Verbiny.

"Well then," said the lady, "Come to this mossy spot for three nights at twelve o'clock, the first night that you come here being two nights before the full moon. You will like it best when the moon is full." And she vanished leaving Verbiny alone.

The next night in Verbiny's dream, Verbiny got up at twelve, and as it was two nights before the full moon Verbiny felt sure that she would see some wonderful things. And indeed she did for in two minutes the lady came in dancing in a circle with a white dress on. The dress looked like cotton and was very lovely. After she had completed seven small circles, she disappeared and Verbiny saw her no more.

Verbiny went home delighted, but she was very curious to know what would happen on the next night. When she went to the mossy spot at twelve she saw the lady in blue, and this time she made six larger circles, and then disappeared as she had before.

When the last night had come Verbiny hurried over to the mossy spot because the lady had said that she would enjoy it most then, and indeed she did, for the lady was dressed in brilliant orange and she was loveliest then. She completed five still larger circles and then went for good. Verbiny lay down on the moss and went to sleep and when she woke up she was sitting in her own bed. "My! but that was a lovely dream," said Verbiny to herself.

In this dream as in the former one, Verbiny escapes from her troubles into magic. Indeed, it could be argued that her lost mother is magically restored to her, and hence that the dream directly compensates for the strained ties with her father. All that this mother-figure does for Verbiny, however, is to weave magic circles at midnight and dazzle her with her costumes of white and blue and orange. The dream supplies magical changes and bright colors; it does not supply maternal warmth, or any comforting glow of feeling. The next day Verbiny tries to apologize to her father, as if to draw closer to him, but he does not hear her; and she must later see him kill a mother watersnake and feed the baby snakes to the ducklings the mother snake was pursuing. There is no end to the dance of death.

In the story of Barbara's life Farksolia functions like one of these dreams, as a means of escape from the troubles and imperfections that oppress her. She makes active use of it for a period of at least four years. But Farksolia is itself infected with typical human troubles. In particular, life there is marred by violence, so much so that the land barely avoids total depopulation. Some fragments of Farksolian history, not dated but presumably written between eight and ten years of age, are preserved in the files of Barbara's writings. From one of these fragments, entitled "Farksolia, the Farksolians, and their details," we learn that Farksolia is a planet about twice the size of the earth, inhabited at one time by people twice as highly developed as those on earth. The manuscript continues:

The Farksolians all agreed, in almost everything. They were all vegetarians, and above anything else they all agreed to live in one big city so that the surrounding landscape would not be spoilt by houses. So that they did, all except a few of the poorer folks. Sheheritzade is the name of the city where they lived. There were eleven queens over Farksolia and all of them were great people. But those queens are grouped in two classes, the queens before Atee, and the queens after Atee. These two groups were of entirely different dispositions. The queens before Atee had their minds always on the goodness of the people, rules that would make them better, and though they all loved ruling and making rules, they all loved beauty also. They could never quite make the people good enough or kind enough and always they tried to make the people as beautiful as the woodlands around the forest, and tried to make the people love these woodlands, and also they tried to make the people love the sea and swim and bathe in it, and rejoice that they were alive. All this the queens before Atee tried to make the people do and be. Then after Atee all was changed. This was during the Farksolian war and so of course all was changed. Queens Lazade, Herazade, Chrysothemis, and Perizade were always urging the warriors on. Such brave men, and such handsome men! They fought hard with the friends of Queen Atee long after Queen Atee herself had passed. But I cannot go on talking about wars and warriors without explaining what it was all about. Queen Atee, the seventh, was chosen because of her beauty, but when she got to ruling the people all decided she was too fierce, turned on the people who had chosen her, and on Queen Atee herself and her friends, and she had many friends. But after the war had passed, the people had overcome Atee, they found themselves extinguished greatly. In fact there were only two families living, with one queen, Perizade, the last. Then Perizade died, and that ended that. The people were sorry that they had gone at Queen Atee at all, and had a hard time struggling along. One family now has a little boy about six years old, and the other family a little girl, about six months. I hope and I want a lot of people to hope with me that the two children may marry and breed the race again.

It is evident from this sketch that Farksolia is not perfect. Vegetarianism has not saved its people from slaughtering one another, and the sensible arrangements and high-principled rules have come to grief on a rebellious spirit aroused by their beautiful but too severe ruler. The last hope lies in a new generation, which may spring from a boy now six and a girl still in the cradle. The boy, we are told in another version of the history, is a genius.

In spite of the bloody history of Farksolia, Barbara often longs to go there. Under date of February 9, 1924, she writes from New Haven to her *"best and dearest friend,"* Mr. St. John:

I would like a little ship to come for me, a little dark green ship with fluttering white sails, laden with my Farksolian friends, for I have some friends of Farksoo and they love me dearly. If they could, they would come for me in the ship that I want. When they got here I would gather up my most precious belongings, and you, dear friend, for you are my best belonging and my most precious. Then we would sail across our ocean and reach an unknown land where some more of my Farksolian friends would be waiting for me with their powerful machine which takes them from one planet to another. Then we would be off for the separate planet. Ah, how wonderful that would be! I wonder what would be the first thing that we should do. I think that the first things I would do would be to stare all around me for ten whole minutes; then I should fall unconsciously on the ground and would be sick for about twenty-four hours which is not the whole of a Farksolian day. I would be sick from breathing the air of the Farksolians, for the air is so different from ours. It is so easy to breathe that an Earthan going to Farksolia would breathe in too much at a time. That is why I should be sick, and I think you would be sick, too. Then I would take you and grip you as though I were afraid of losing you, and we would wander out from the city of Sheheritzade into the open fields. Then we would lie down together and gaze from the soft green emerald grass to the sapphire sky, where we should see the swallow-like birds circling. Then I should look a little lower and would see the butterflies. Then I would look down in the grass around me and would see the dear little busy insects visiting first one flower, then another. We would watch the golden butterflies going everywhere on soft, silent, golden wings. The wind would bear them through the sapphire sky over us, and under us would be the rich brown Earth of Farksolia. I would feel the soft green grass all up my back and would smell of all the flowers coming within reach of my happy nostrils. We would breathe in great breaths of the warm scented air. How happy we would be. I think that we would be perfectly contented to stay there all day without eating a morsel. Then when dusk came on we would wander into the city again and dine on silvery fruits of marvellous tastes. Then at night we would gaze from the meadow again into the wonderful night sky of a mixture of ultramarine and black. We would see the constellation called "Peen Flitterveen." It has this name because it is shaped exactly like a big butterfly with beautiful curving lines of stars for the feelers. And a curious thing about this constellation is that all the stars in it are of a golden colour. Then we would also see the other important constellation called "Peen Farksiades." That constellation hasn't a very remarkable pattern, but the stars. They are remarkable because they are black, little black stars! Oh, how lovely they are, though they are very inconspicuous against the ultramarine and black night sky! My, but they are lovely! Then we should also see the two moons of Farksolia and their names are Vaireen and Seeven. Vaireen is rather like our moon in colouring, but Seeven is very inconspicuous for it is nearly the colour of the day sky in the day and the night sky at night. But both the moons are very lovely. Do you think that this is a very true description of what we would do if we went to Farksolia? I do.

Very lovingly,
Barbara.

Of the same date is a letter to Mr. Oberg soliciting his co-operation in illustrating a book on Farksolia. It contains the following passage:

FARKSOO! FARKSOLIA! Harrah! Would that the greatest people in the universe would let down their mighty machine which will take them to other planets and take us to their planet Farksolia. Ah, wouldn't that be wonderful? I wonder how you would like it, for though it is beautiful it is very peculiar and strange in almost every way. It is

> Where the skies are bluest,
> Where the leaves are green,
> Where the white-capped wavelets
> Glisten with shimmery sheen.
>
> Where the waves come rolling in,
> Where a song of the sea is heard,
> Where the goddess Virodine
> Leaps to the song of a bird.
>
> Where the skies are black and blue,
> Where the stars are shining white,
> Where the blackened billows
> Thunder with terrible might.
>
> Where the grass is soft and green
> Where the flowers bloom;

Where the billows blue once more
Mightily do boom.

Where the flower stars are shining,
Where the wind-borne butterflies
Do silently sail
Through the sapphire skies.

This is like Farksolia with a sea more wonderful than any Earthan thing, and where more lovely butterflies than ever dreamed of on Earth sail wind-borne through the sapphire skies. Ah, Farksolia is surely a wonderful place with its booming billows thundering against high cliffs. I should like a little ship with white fluttering sails to come for me loaded with my Farksoo friends, for I have some friends of Farksoo and they love me dearly. They, if they could, would come for me in the ship that I want. It has a green ship part and the rest would be fluttering sails. They would come for me if they could, and I would gather my precious belongings and then we would be off! Through the waves of our sea we would gently glide and then we would reach an unknown land where the other Farksolians would be waiting for us with that powerful machine and then we would be off for Farksolia! Through the foaming dashing waves we would go with a silent gliding motion and when we got to the unknown land we would be off for Farksolia! And if I ever came back, which would be doubtful, I would never be contented with the Earth again.

What makes Farksolia so attractive to Barbara? Basically, it seems very much like the earth, with its fields and its forests, with its seas and skies, with its birds, butterflies, and stars. What advantage does it have over the earth? Can it possibly be that the advantage lies in the most terrible aspect of its history? The destructive wars beginning with the rebellion against Queen Atee had the successful, though extremely costly, outcome that they rid the country of all rulers; the future lies with two children, a genius of six and a baby, who may grow up and marry and reproduce, untroubled by the interference of powerful adults belonging to the old royal line. This Farksolian situation is consonant with many of

[52]

Barbara's stories. In spite of the affection which she manifests in her letters to Mr. Oberg, Mr. St. John, and "dear Daddy-Dog," and in her accounts of her baby sister, she often writes about escaping from parents or other adults, and at times from all human beings.

One way of escape is by magic and the fairies. "The Adventures of Curis" and "Evandine" are two stories from the Farksolian period that use this device. In "Evandine" the escape is total. That will be considered in a moment. In "The Adventures of Curis" the escape is partial and tentative. Curis, having overheard her mother and father at night discussing a field of gold, resolves to find the field and bring back some of the gold for her mother, who is poor. She succeeds in this venture and deposits a wagonload of gold at her mother's door. She next goes wandering off to find a field of mixed flowers; in this she has the aid of a man who gives her a daisy, to warn her magically against a monster living in the water pipes and to guide her to fairyland and to the fairies who give her the final directions. In the field of mixed flowers she stays for some time, loving the flowers and the chipmunks, squirrels, bees, butterflies, and birds, especially the hummingbirds, *"and soon they came when she whistled to them or called, and that was the*

Butterfly illustrations for projected book on Farksoli painted by Mr. Oberg to Barbara's minute specifications

treasure she had been seeking." When she returns home, she is greeted by reproaches from her mother for going away without telling her. Curis explains that she herself didn't know she was going until she met the man with the magic flower. Her mother asks her what use a field of mixed flowers is anyway. Her answer is that more than anything else she loves flowers, and chipmunks, birds, bees, and butterflies, which now come to her whenever she calls them. Her mother thinks that she would be better employed in getting gold, but is somewhat mollified when Curis offers to take her to fairyland. On their expedition, Curis proves to be much more knowledgeable about fairyland than her mother, who in fact is rather uninformed and stupid. While they are away robbers come to the house and steal the gold; they even go to the field of gold and deplete it of its reserves. But they meet their proper retribution: they are devoured by the monster in the water pipes; and the fairies, it seems, can be counted on to restore the gold losses. Once again Curis sets forth for fairyland, requesting her magic flower of the man who keeps it and asking him how to get to the Land of Butterflies where, she is told, one may be crowned with butterflies *"but as soon as anyone takes a step out of the Land of Butterflies the crown just flies away."* Upon her arrival there:

Right off she was crowned with yellow butterflies. She called to the butterflies, and it seemed to her as if she was buried in a yellow mist; all the butterflies in that section of the land were there. Curis sang:

   "Butterflies, butterflies, back away,
     You bury me in yellow ray."
All at once the butterflies understood, they backed away making room for Curis to kneel down. Then Curis sang:
   "Butterflies, butterflies, come to me,
     Yellow butterflies full of glee."
The butterflies all came into Curis's lap, where they fluttered about. Curis said: "You sweet little butterflies, I am so glad I came to The Land of Butterflies." All at once the fairies came into that land. They danced around Curis and the butterflies, sweetly. Curis felt that her mother must be searching for her, and she felt resolved

to go home, but she didn't want to in the least. She sang:
"Oh fairies oh fairies, I must go home,
Mother will be afraid of my roam."

A worried mother greets her on her return, and when Curis asks her why she is so inquisitive about the Land of Butterflies, her mother calls her *"dreadfully rude,"* and adds, *"I don't like the way you act at all."* Curis retorts in kind: *"Well, you are so inquisitive, I don't like the way you act either."* Curis then scampers off to return her flower to the man, and the man quite agrees with her (and against her mother) in regard to the beauty of the Land of Butterflies and the appropriateness of its name. Again she returns home:

When Curis got home, her mother was nearly sobbing, for she had been away once more in her life without telling her mother first, and even then, she had given back the flower, and her mother was awfully worried. She said: "You naughty little thing, you don't know that you are in danger of losing your life, just because you left your flower somewhere."

In a conciliatory mood Curis explains that when she wants the flower again for passing over dangerous terrain she can get it by asking the man for it, and she even agrees to let her mother get it for her occasionally. But after lengthy reflection alone in her room, she changes her mind; and so the next day, without telling her mother, she returns to the man and gets her flower for another trip to fairyland:

When her mother got round to going over, the man said: "Miss Curis has taken the flower so you can't have it until Miss Curis gives it back to me."

"Miss Curis is my daughter," said Curis's mother, "she told me that I could go and get it for her, she is a little wretch, is Curis."

"Not a bit of a wretch," said the man, "she is a good, kind girl, and I think that I will never let you have the flower, I don't like the way you act."

Of course Curis's mother felt hurt about it.

Curis does not permanently leave home. There is tension between her and her mother, and she has much more sympathetic rapport with the man who handles the flower and with the non-human inhabitants of fairyland; but there is no final rupture, merely friction.

In the story "Evandine," on the other hand, the rupture is complete. This story, which has touches of the Farksoo language, is in many ways a direct anticipation of Barbara's book, *The House Without Windows*, published by Knopf in 1927. It runs to eight pages, broken into six chapters. In the first chapter, we find Evandine waking up tired and cross early in the morning. But a fairy comes by and touches her, *"muttering strange charms."* Dressed in her prettiest dress, with a bow at the back like a butterfly, Evandine trips out of the house and along the garden path. There she discovers that she can sail through the air, at first in long leaps, and then with more and more freedom, until she is hovering and diving like a swallow. The second chapter introduces the concern of her parents:

But, of course, such happy things cannot go on forever without an interruption. While she was swooping and swerving and having the time of her life let us return to Eezanne's parents, Mr. and Mrs. Foresteen. Naturally they missed her. She was usually up early anyhow, and they were surprised not to find her up and down-stairs. So, after waiting a little while, Mrs. Foresteen went up to her room to see what was going on there.

A cry of terror escaped her lips. "Charles," she cried, "Charles,— she is not here!"

"Not here," said Mr. Foresteen aghast, coming into the room.

"NO," she said. "I've searched everywhere—and I've looked down in the garden, and she isn't—she isn't."

A sound like the call of a bird was heard, and, a moment later, Eezanne rushed by the window, laughing.

"Oh," said Mrs. Foresteen, "oh, Eezanne, come here, my child! How do you do it?"

A laugh like the tinkling of bells was the answer, and an armful of strange-smelling, beautiful flowers glided down through the window from nowhere. She was not seen again, but at frequent intervals that strange cry was heard.

Mr. and Mrs. Foresteen could do nothing but gaze at each other.

Mrs. Foresteen's gentle face was full of love and delight, but that of her husband was full of anger.

"How dare she," he said angrily, "how dare she? The impudent rascal."

"No, no," said Mary (Mrs. Foresteen). "Do not take her away. The fairies have touched her. She has doings with Nature, and she will stay about the house, or at least, visit us occasionally, and cheer us. But no, we must not touch her. We must not take her away from her happy life with Nature and with the fairies.

"But goodness, Charles, how lovely she is. Did you see how gracefully she swooped about?"

"Yes," said Mr. Foresteen, still angrily. "Lovely she may be. But this cannot go on. She cannot stay. Think of cold nights, and cold days, and—er—er—snow-storms, and all else. And, dearest, her party dress. And, no education, and—er—starvation and—and death!"

"Yes, Charles," answered Mrs. Foresteen, "but, dearest, she has been touched by the fairies to keep her from cold nights and cold days and snow-storms, together with all dangers such as starvation and death. And—er—education? What of that? What is education compared with such a sacred life with Nature and the fairies, and the butterflies and bees (which are Nature) and all the other lovely things which she now has? Think how much happier she now is than she would be with school-teachers, lead-pencils, other school-children, arithmetic, French, history? I have always wondered what to do with her. I have always hated to send her to school, for she is not the kind of child for school. Here it is decided for me. Here I have a splendid opportunity to let my child have all the loveliest things. Shall I let it go by? Certainly not! Is that quite clear to you, Charles?"

"I—I guess so Mary."

"Then, are we at peace with each other?"

"Heaven grant it true."

Eezanne (or Evandine) flits among the flowers, sipping their nectar and singing, at times flying about her mother's head; then she drops some bright red blossoms in her mother's lap and swoops off. Later, she flies out over the ocean and, looking down at it, *"all blue, green, and silver, with the sun dancing on its smooth, yet wavy surface,"* she calls to it, *"Oh, Mother!"* Thereupon, because it has been so decreed, the charm which enables her to fly is broken and she falls into the sea, where the sea-fairies keep her. Now the Foresteens have to move down beside the sea in order to watch their daughter, dressed and crowned in seaweed, ride the highest waves with perfect aplomb. (*"Her parents watched her with delighted faces, for hours."*) Of this delight, too, there is an end. And the final chapter says:

Wings again! Wings again! That was what Eezanne called all day and all night. The sea was nice, the sea was wonderful, but Eezanne, with sadness in her heart, remembered the time when she could fly, when she could swoop through the air like a swallow. Her sea-weeds looked more and more bedraggled. She ceased to play with the big waves. She lay stretched out in all the beauty around. She liked to watch the gulls circling above her head, yet it only made her sadder. She tried to forget it, but could not.

There were a few mischievous fairies that did not wish her to fly again. These were the fairies of the sea. They wanted little Eezanne to stay with them and be happy. She stayed with them, but was not happy. At last the air fairies took great pity on her, and the sea fairies saw that it was necessary to let her go. And so they released their tight grip on her, and one beautiful day, she rose from the waves, shook herself clear of the flying spray, and sailed out through the sky, dressed in rose-petals of pink and white.

After this she spent all her time in the air, even sleeping, with nothing under. Some say she never touched the ground again. This I cannot say, but I know that she was happy all the rest of her life. Perhaps she turned into a seagull.

And so Evandine, as a human being, disappears—to become perhaps a seagull, but also perhaps a butterfly or moth, for a poem appended to the story concludes:

She rises from the sea clothed in rose petals,
And two strong, white wings.
Like a moth from a cocoon,

She wakes from a life in the sea,
Into the air again.

At this period most of Barbara's stories are concerned with beauty and sensory pleasure and with the theme of magical escape. Rare is the story that does not employ magic and that stays within the bounds of the human, focusing on human relationships rather than on Nature. A conspicuous example of this rare variety is one entitled "A Little Girl," or "Maireena." This too is a story of escape from adult supervision, but the escape is accomplished by the death of the adults; and it contains more evidence of tragic emotion than is usual in Barbara's work. Succinctly, a girl named Maireena loses her father and blind grandmother by death, and simultaneously is parted from a girl friend because of the death of the friend's father, a doctor who attended Maireena's father during his last illness. She has no other relatives or friends, and so, *"deserted by all mankind,"* she is left alone with her pony, Starre: *"She went into the barn where Starre and Snow-white were feeding quietly. 'Starre,' she said, 'Starre.' The horse looked up. 'Starre,' she said, 'you are my only friend—the only one I have to love, and the only one that loves me—for you love me, don't you Starre?' "*
The way in which Maireena's needs and emotions are handled in this melancholy story may help us to understand what is going on in the more magical tales, and even why it is that Barbara courts the idea of departing entirely from earthly life. The focal event in the story is clearly the death of Maireena's father, and it is evident that Maireena is greatly attached to him in spite of the fact that *"Her father was very busy and so she was left to herself a good deal of the time."* In her loneliness she takes pleasure in slipping away to the small barn where two horses are stalled, one of them her own. It is her habit to feed the horse *"some little pieces of corn or an apple or two,"* and then climb up through the hayloft to a secret passage leading to *"a windowless, dark, close, crowded storeroom"* where she can employ her time in rummaging about *"among the dusty old furniture,"* sometimes *"discovering strange old jewels or old coins, one of which had been coined in Joan of Arc's time. It had a hole in the centre and Maireena wore it around her neck, for*

Joan was her favorite heroine." It would appear that Maireena's solitary occupations are not so much preferred by her as required by the fact of her father's absence. One day, when she is up in the hayloft, she has the impulse to ride Starre into the city to meet her father. On arriving at his office, only half a mile from her home, she is shocked to learn that he has already left and has been gone an hour. "*Of course if he had left an hour ago he would be home by this time, for certainly it would not take an hour for a strong, healthy man to walk half a mile.*" It occurs to her, as a comforting thought, that he may have gone into the center of town, five miles away, to make some purchases needed for his work. She goes in search of him there and finds him, but, again with a shock, discovers that he is seriously ill. She hurries off to fetch the doctor. Her father is removed by the doctor to the hospital: "*She and Starre galloped home, Maireena thinking sadly: 'Oh, if Daddy dies what shall I do?' She put Starre in her stall, but took no pleasure in it, as she usually did. She meant to go to her grandmother, tell her her story, then hear some of grandmother's stories, and try to forget her own.*" She is diverted from this intention for several hours by a big yellow cat and her newborn kittens, with whom she plays in the hayloft. The next morning she sets out to see the doctor who has been so kind to her father. She bids farewell to her grandmother, whom she leaves in a state of great anxiety, choked with tears. Maireena, however, does not spend the day with the doctor or her father. Instead, she invites the doctor's daughter, Katherine, to ride with her a little while in the country, and Katherine's company is so entrancing that the whole day is devoted to her entertainment, riding the horses, playing in the barn with the kittens, searching through the dusty storeroom and finding there beautiful ancient costumes and other treasures, such as a plain gold ring engraved "1351" and a tiny golden goblet inscribed with the name of an ancestor,

> "*Sabrina Medici Vendras*
> *In the year*
> *1670.*"

In token of their warm friendship, Maireena quite overwhelms Katherine with the gift of a kitten:

"Oh," Katherine gasped, "oh, you can't, you don't love me as much as that, you are mocking me." (She thought of many things to say, but none of them came out well enough.)

"Of course I'm not mocking you," Maireena said indignantly.

She was going on when she saw a hurricane of gratitude forming on Katherine's face, but understanding what a strain she was going through she simply said, kindly: "I know. I feel that way often when I'm being given anything. Don't trouble to thank me. I know just how you feel."

Those soft comforting words wound themselves upon Katherine like water on parched flowers: "You darling," she cried, "I love you, I do. You are my very, very best friend. Oh, I cannot tell you how grateful I am!"

It is significant that Barbara, in working over this piece of writing, ran her censoring editorial pencil through the above passage, as well as some others in which emotion was expressed. The tendency to rule emotion out is evident within the story itself: the heroine's chief stratagem in dealing with the most powerful emotions is to hide them and seek diversion in other thoughts or in concealing actions. Most of the chapter following the above, for instance, in the midst of her father's illness, is taken up with how Maireena provides her new friend with gifts and advice (on making the most of an ugly horse Katherine has acquired) and invites her over for another visit. Yet, inserted into the middle of the chapter is the information that Maireena's father is much worse, and it is stated at the end that "*a sad thought kept pulling at her heart, that —but she tried to think of something else.*" The scene in the middle of the chapter is especially instructive:

Dr. Fisher was just going out and he met them in the hall. Maireena inquired with her heart thumping wildly. Dr. Fisher held her close as he said:

"Your poor dear father is much worse, we think that he has not an hour to live, and—"

But Maireena tore herself loose, shut the door with a pretty hard bang, unhitched Starre, and said not a word to Katherine.

[61]

Maireena's self-control is formidable. The whole remainder of that day until late at night, except the time taken for meals, is spent by the two friends playing in the barn loft, exploiting the possibilities in old trunks of dresses and other dusty things for pretending that they are queens and princesses. They go to great pains to rearrange the stored furniture (with the aid of Katherine's older brother, Charles), and never give a thought to the dying father.

The final chapter is entitled "Sadness in its True Form." It begins: "*In the morning they ate a hearty breakfast and then—alas! I wish Maireena hadn't thought of her father. If she hadn't this joy in the hayloft would have gone on forever.*" Maireena wildly upbraids herself for forgetting him, and for being happy while he lies dying or is perhaps already dead. (After all, the doctor told her the morning before that her father might not live an hour.) She mounts her horse and gallops off to the hospital, where she learns that her father is indeed dead. After a wild shriek of grief, she tears herself away from the doctor and starts to leave; but he detains her a moment with the interesting information that she must look for something hidden in the hayloft wall. This proves to be a fortune of $3,000,000. She tells her grandmother about it, and:

All day they talked together, and when evening came they went to bed early. In the morning she rose and, to her great dismay she found poor old grandmother, lying peacefully on the bed, dead. And that same fateful day Charles, ignorant in the fact that grandmother was dead, telephoned to Maireena that doctor had suddenly been smitten by a terrible illness and he had died and that he and Katherine were going with their aunt across to France. Then, indeed Maireena felt herself deserted by all mankind.

There immediately follows Maireena's appeal to her horse as the only being left in the world to love her.

One must be impressed by the centrality of the theme of death in this story by a very young girl. One must also be impressed by the heroine's manner of dealing with her emotions. She tries to ride down the most disturbing fact of her experience—the death of her father—by the games and pretense with which she fills up the lonely hours, and she does not, when in the arms of the kindly doctor, pour out her grief to him and seek some relief in human sympathy: no, she tears herself away from him, shuts the door with a bang, and becomes silent. How much of Maireena is an image of Barbara?

Chapter IV

Barbara's first published book was brought out early in 1927 by Knopf. This was *The House Without Windows and Eepersip's Life There*. A note written by her father and appended to the story outlines the history of its production. As he informs us, Barbara wrote the story in its first version as a gift to her mother on the occasion of Barbara's own ninth birthday in March of 1923. Later, her father suggested that she might clean up the manuscript a bit and get a few copies of it printed for her friends. She accordingly spent the summer months of 1923 at Lake Sunapee in what was meant to be a final polishing of her work. She brought it home to New Haven with her in October. A night later, fire broke out in the house, and the manuscript was destroyed in the general destruction of the house and its contents. Barbara then set herself to the difficult task of reproducing the lost story. She toiled away along this line for several weeks.

Then, one day in December, everything was suddenly different. As an experiment of despair, Barbara had stopped trying to remember the shape of sentences, the precise order and phraseology of details, and had begun to let the material come back as it listed. And to her astonishment it came in a freshet, like northern rivers when the ice goes out. When, a few days later, we put work aside to organize our makeshift Christmas, she was still in a happy glow, the first third of the fantasy existed again, and the story was running over its banks.

There followed one interruption after another, and it was not until the autumn of 1924 that the second draft was completed. In the late winter of 1924–25, Barbara worked patiently through the first third, putting it in what she hoped would be final shape. The manuscript had to be laid away in May of 1925, and was not touched again for nine months. Then, in February and March, 1926, she did her revision of the second and third parts, made a few minor improvements in Part I, and typed out a fair copy of the whole —the copy from which this little book is set.[1]

It is stated in her father's note that the final manuscript was in all essentials like the original, but with more elaboration of the Fleuriss episode, which concerns Eepersip's kidnaping of her younger sister from her parents.

> The obvious reason for this is that the author's own young sister, at the time of the first draft, existed only as an insistent demand on Barbara's part; whereas in the period of the revision she was a dream fulfilled, subject to adoring daily observation.[2]

The decision that the book should be commercially published, rather than simply "manufactured," was one which gradually took shape in Mr. Follett's mind, his view being that the story was, to quote him,

> . . . valuable . . . as a representation of something lovely in generalized childhood itself—and yet not so very likely to achieve frequent expression. The fact is that the impulses crystallized in this story mostly fade into the light of common day a year or two before the dawn of that amount of mechanical articulacy which is necessary for a tangible expression of them; and they are therefore almost never expressed. Actually, I do not happen to be acquainted with a single prose document of much scope which achieves the full expression, or any first-hand expression, of what is in a normal, healthy child's mind and heart during that mysterious phase when butterflies, flowers, winging swallows, and white-capped waves are twice as real as even a quite bearable parent, and incomparably more important. . . .[3]

[1] "Historical Note," by Wilson Follett, pp. 159–60 in Barbara Newhall Follett, *The House Without Windows and Eepersip's Life There* (New York: Knopf, 1927).

[2] *Ibid.*, p. 126.

[3] *Ibid.*, pp. 163–64.

In setting down the above assessment of the value of the story, Mr. Follett clearly had in mind the poetic descriptions and rapt adoration of Nature that make up a large part of *The House Without Windows*. The young author herself, however, emphasized the human core of it rather than the natural scenery. For her, it was primarily a story of a child who *"ran away from loneliness,"* as she phrased it in a letter of February 13, 1925. Earlier, in a letter to Mr. St. John of February 4, 1923, when she was beginning work on the first version, she wrote: *"It is about a little girl named Eepersip who lived on top of a mountain, Mount Varcrobis, and was so lonely that she went away to live wild."* And further: *"She talked to the animals, and led a sweet lovely life with them—just the kind of life that I should like to lead. Her parents all tried to catch her, with some friends of theirs, and every time she escaped in some way or other."*

The House Without Windows is a story of escape. The little runaway escapes first into the meadows near home and lives with the deer and other animals; later, into the sea; and finally, into the mountains among the eternal snows, quite alone, without the companionship of even a single animal, until at last a flurry of butterflies carries her away into invisibility.

That day Eepersip was even happier than usual. She floated about, visiting each flower, each bush and tree. She played games with the butterflies, the games she had played on the old meadow, that first summer of her life in the House without Windows. When she rested, she sat on top of a laurel-bush, and not a twig bent beneath her. The slightest breeze blew her about, changed the direction of her dance. Butterfly after butterfly flew to her, flock after flock, as if they had some message to tell her; and after each visit she was happier than before. Yes, they were messengers, these happy creatures; messengers who came to whisper her a secret—a secret from Nature, a secret of the beautiful meadow, a secret from the fairies.

And, when the sun again tinged the sky with colour, a flock of these butterflies, of purple and gold and green, came swooping and alighted on her head in a circle, the largest in front. Others came in myriads and covered her dress with delicate wing-touches. Eepersip held out her arms a moment. A gold-and-black one alighted on each wrist. And then—she rose into the air, and, hovering an instant over a great laurel-bush, vanished.

She was a fairy—a wood-nymph. She would be invisible forever to all mortals, save those few who have minds to believe, eyes to see. To these she is ever present, the spirit of Nature—a sprite of the meadow, a naiad of lakes, a nymph of the woods.[4]

So ends the story on which Barbara had lavished so much attention between her ninth birthday and her thirteenth. She had consulted her father with regard to the first version, as to whether he thought it would please her mother; and their collaboration had continued during the following years. His reaction to her question when he first saw what she had done was that it would indeed please her mother, and he joined to that his own enthusiasm.

I liked it myself, if only as unconscious expression of a radiant physical vitality—so much I found in it of the mighty swimmer, the enjoyable young comrade of trail and river, always ready to swing a paddle tirelessly or carry ungrumbling a fair share of pack. I liked it, too, as her answer to the one year which she had ever been called upon to spend in undeniably tawdry surroundings.[5]

The tawdry surroundings here referred to were the rooms of the rented apartment that they were occupying this year. Barbara did not like the place, it is true. She bursts out in a letter to Mr. St. John (February 4, 1923):

I want as long as possible in that green, fairylike, woodsy, animal-filled, watery, luxuriant, butterfly-painted, moth-dotted, dragonfly-blotched, bird-filled, salamandrous, mossy, ferny, sunshiny, moon-shiny, long-dayful, short-nightful land, on that fishy, froggy, tadpoly, shelly, lizard-filled lake—oh, no end of lovely things to say

[4] Ibid., pp. 152–53.
[5] Ibid., pp. 156–57.

about that place, and I am mad to get there. I want as short a time as possible in this vile apartment house—oh, anywhere, everywhere except here!

Lake Sunapee is the haven on which she scatters the blessing of this armful of epithets, and no doubt in writing the story at this very time she was recapturing some of its green magic; but, as the history of Barbara's literary development shows and as she herself states in this letter, the story that was to become *The House Without Windows* began *"long, long ago,"* long before they ever entered the apartment, and cannot adequately be understood simply as a reaction to confinement there. It is the culmination of the escape theme present in many other, earlier stories. Probably the drab apartment gave an extra push. Still, it may have been less that factor than a new, deeper engagement with the problem of human greed and violence that energized this supreme effort to withdraw from mankind and fuse with Nature. She pours her heart out to Mr. St. John in her long letter of January 23, 1923, which must be close to the beginning date of Eepersip:

I shall have to try you a little more with a new subject now, that will take centuries to straighten out—really a great subject—that, besides writing to you my feeling, I will discuss with you when I see you in New Hampshire, on Lake Sunapee.

Everything is now (except human beings) just as Nature has planned it. Nature did not plan her children to be killed, except sometimes by one another, but she planned them to live and enjoy the earth—the sunlight, the flowers, the trees, and all Nature's beauties. If only we mortals will wake up and learn a lesson, here is a lesson for us to learn. As Nature has not planned her children to be killed, why do we kill them? Who can answer this question? Nature has trusted to us, animals' big brothers and sisters, to leave her babies alone. If only some of us could wake up and be brought to see the right side of this very complicated subject, they would think, the way I do, of the person who gets wounded, what he feels like, and how his feelings are hurt. Why do we kill pigs for pork or ham? why do we kill cows for beef? or lambs for their meat? When we kill the animals we are not doing what Nature has planned; whereas the animals do what Nature has planned, no matter what this may be.

Volcanoes that spout up ash and kill plants near by cannot help it, for Nature has planned it; worms we hate because they are ugly—they do nobody any harm, and they cannot help how they look, for Nature has planned it; and the plants they kill we needn't blame them for, for Nature has planned it; eagles, falcons, and hawks cannot help killing and eating smaller birds, for that is their nature, and that is what the real Nature has put in them. Old Mother Nature must have some bad animals as well as some good ones, or the world would never get along. But I don't think she needs us. For my part I think that we mortals should be cleared off the earth entirely—I shouldn't mind being cleared off, because I know what harm we do.

How one can look at the fuzzy yellow ball of a little chicken and then want to kill it is more than I can see—even for Easter, which some people think is more important than the lives of chickens. The chicken never did anybody any harm; it is human greed that makes us kill them. I could never see how anyone can do such a thing. How one can look into the gentle loving eyes of a deer and then want to kill him, I can't understand. Perhaps it would be all right to kill a few, for the earth would soon be overrun with them if we didn't, but why should North America all over have the same seasons for killing deer? You know in some places this season comes in the mating time. My idea is that every different climate should have an open season that doesn't come in the mating time. How one can want to shoot ducks is also more than I can see, even for the good meat. They never did anybody any harm, and probably never will. It is only human greed.

Now animals like horses, cows, donkeys, and bees are meant to serve man: the horses and donkeys to carry burdens, the cows to give us milk, and the bees to give us honey. But if man could only be contented with all these luxuries! It doesn't hurt these slaves of ours to serve us, for that is what Nature has planned, but Nature has not planned minks, beavers, seals, bears, skunks, and muskrats to serve us, and, therefore, it hurts them. For we take their skins.

Nature has not planned naughty boys to throw stones at chipmunks, squirrels, and birds; Nature has not planned us to catch fishes and eat them (something which even I do); Nature has not planned naughty boys to catch lizards or salamanders with crooked pins (something which I cannot bear to think about).

Now about butterflies. If we could only be brought to see as I do. Why do people have to know exactly where every spot on a butterfly's wing is? There is no need to make collections of butterflies, for why do we have to know just exactly about them? Human beings are so fussy! Much the better way of finding out about butterflies is to catch them and put them in a sieve and describe them. I think that it is much better not to get their description exact and to let the butterfly live on, in its lovely life, than to kill and get everything exact. This is what I do, and I hope that you think it is better as well as I. Butterflies live such lovely lives and are such lovely things that I couldn't think of killing them. I simply love them!

Now again, I can't understand how a boy with any heart at all can bear to take little birds out of their nests. Jays and crows that steal the nests we hate, but it is their nature and they can not help it.

Now again I don't see how anyone can bear to see flowers die in the heat of a train—I'm sure I can't.

In other words I am a friend of all Nature save human beings, and for this reason can be brought to see the right side of things.

I, when I see you again, will talk over this subject with you thoroughly, for to me it is very important.

Barbara's general thought—that beautiful and precious living things are in danger because of the greed of human beings—obtains vivid expression in a story which she was working at in the midst of her struggles to rewrite *The House Without Windows*. In this other story, one gets the impression of visiting the depths of the Jungian Collective Unconscious and coming up against the most basic instincts and archetypes. The hero and heroine, Sarbea and Chrysothemis, do not hesitate to use violence to protect what they value. By contrast, Eepersip is ethereal. Barbara thus appears to exist at this time between two poles—the violent underworld, and the airy elusiveness of Eepersip and her fairies.

The close association between the two stories can be gathered from this portion of a letter to her grandmother, *"My own dear Ding,"* of November 24, 1923:

After we had the fire all my hopes were concentrated on the remaining chance that Eepersip was to come by express with my books. But that chance, too, disappeared mercilessly. Eepersip was lost! One day I tried very hard to rewrite, but I couldn't get more than half a page done. So I gave it up and started an entirely new story called The Great Labyrinth of Sarbea. Sarbea is the hero of the story—he is the son of a poor couple that lived by the sea. They had in their possession a great blue pearl about the size of a hen's egg. When they died they handed it over to Sarbea, who, with the aid of the queen of the country, found his way to an uninhabited island and built for its keeping a great labyrinth all doors, doors, rooms, large and small, and a great tangle of passages, long and short. Sarbea found an enchantress who got for him some great dragons who guarded the labyrinth a dragon standing at all of the entrances and nearly all of the main passages inside. Many folks from neighboring islands strove for the pearl, but always at a great loss. After the labyrinth was built Sarbea returned from the island to his own land and, also with the aid of the queen, and at the same time against the will of the king married the beautiful princess, Chrysothemis. Then husband and wife returned to the uninhabited island where they built a little cottage and where Chrysothemis worked very diligently in a beautiful garden she was making every day.

In the middle of this new story I had an inspiration, a very sudden inspiration, it came to me while I was working on The Great Labyrinth of Sarbea, and I turned the page out quick as a wink, put in a fresh one and wrote on the top of it: "The Adventures of Eepersip," and worked on it like fire for four pages. It is turning out to be a much better story than the first. . . .

The summary of the labyrinth story in the letter refers to the first thirteen pages of the manuscript. Evidently, though it is incomplete, she worked at it further, since in its present form it runs to nineteen pages. The following excerpts will serve to give body to Barbara's summary and make clear the preciousness of the pearl, the elaborateness of the protective measures, and the degree of violence and ingenuity exercised in caring for it. The story begins:

By the shore of the sea there lived a man and his wife. They were very poor, but they were very happy for they had one treasure which might make them rich if they had cared to part with it. This treasure was a pearl, a single solitary pearl, but a remarkable pearl it was, being about the size of a hen's egg of a deep blue colour, and it shimmered with all the blues in the world. This pearl was proof to everything except what might crush it, even fire could not tarnish it in the least. The only thought that concerned them was about that pearl after their death. They did not want wicked people to have it; they wanted to have a child to pass it down to.

Day after day went by and at last a little son was born to them and oh how glad they were! A long time passed and the boy was playing in the sand on the beach, and watching the little hermit crabs playing in the tide pools at high tide. There was never a happier boy.

When he was eleven years old his father thought that it would be best to tell him a little about the great pearl that had for so long been their dearest treasure, only excepting the son himself. They told him that when they were dead he must always keep it very carefully, and sometime before he was too old to defend it properly he must build it a hiding-place, where until its walls rotted away no one might get it. Thus they told the boy Sarbea, for that was his name. "And if you marry," said his Mother, Mrs. Labina, "You had better marry a woman younger than you are."

When his parents die, Sarbea takes the pearl in his hand and goes to the palace of the king. It is from the queen, however, that he seeks and obtains assistance. A ship is provisioned; a crew of builders, an enchantress, and dragons are put aboard; and after many days on the sea and in the face of storms, Sarbea and his forces come to an uninhabited island. Here they immediately set to work to construct a hiding-place for the pearl:

The day after they had landed the constructors began the work of building a great labyrinth. And very large it was, for it covered a square half-mile of land. They felled great trees which disappeared like lightning. At last, in about three years of heavy work the great labyrinth was finished, meanwhile the men had been getting their dinners at the close island Myrolon. According to Sarbea's orders the constructors had built in the very middle of the great building a little tiny room, with four doors and at each door a dragon was to stand. Each door had a long passage leading to it from the outside, three of these passages had doors without keys, but the fourth passage was the way Sarbea was to visit his beloved treasure which of course was in the little room. The doors from the outside of the building to the tiny room were all locked, and a terrible dragon stood at each door of that passage. The four doors of the little room were also locked. From the outside of the labyrinth there were at least a hundred and twenty doors, but only one of these was locked, this was the door which led into Sarbea's passage. But a dragon stood at every one of the outside entrances. At last the great building was finished, the dragons stood in their places, a dragon guarding nearly every main passage, the pearl was in the little room, and the enchantress had a great spider spin webs around it. It was all passage was the way Sarbea was to visit his beloved treasure which of led into a big room with doors all around it. Some of these doors led into passages and some into rooms, all surrounded with doors. There were over a million doors in the labyrinth, and one would never know whether or when one was going to meet one of those dread dragons, against whom no four people could stand. But they were always nice to Sarbea when he came down his passage to look at his beloved pearl.

That work completed, Sarbea returns to the palace of the king and, once more with the aid of the queen, approaches and wins the love of Chrysothemis, the princess. The queen allows him to enter her bedroom while she is still asleep:

Very gently he opened the door and walked in, and oh, what a glorious sight met his eyes. The door revealed a large room the walls of which were pure ivory. The ceiling was curved and two great ivory pillars were ornamented with jewels. On the floors was spread a great fleecy white rug. Most of the furniture was white but not ivory. There were several chairs, a bureau on which was set a bouquet of purple and white violets, and a large couch on which lay Chrysothemis, the beautiful princess. Sarbea stared all around him in amazement of what he saw. Then, when he recovered his wits a little, he drew a small chair up to the couch, sat down upon it, and watched over Chrysothemis.

For three quarters of an hour Sarbea sat there motionless drinking in her sheer beauty, but at last she woke and started for joy when she saw him. "Ah," she said, "you were the one I loved."

Aware of the opposition to be expected from the king her father, the two lovers discuss means of marrying and escaping without his knowledge. They are aided in their designs by the queen. The king is got out of the way by a ruse while the wedding takes place, but he returns in time to see the bride and groom departing in their ship and immediately sets out in angry pursuit with his own ship. Pursuer and pursued race across the sea. At last, Sarbea reaches the island of the labyrinth. The king arrives simultaneously. There is too little time for Sarbea's party to enter the stoutly fortified labyrinth:

Chrysothemis just had time to duck under the outstretched arm of the captain dragon, the dragon that guarded Sarbea's passage, while Sarbea and the eighteen men leant up against the walls and prepared to fight. Chrysothemis was guarding this dragon and the dragon was guarding her. This is the way in which she succeeded in saving him from many a hard thrust with an enemy's sword. She drew her own bright silver glistening little blade and made thrusts around the dragon in all directions so that it was difficult for any man to come too close. But by quite a while she began to think her strokes were of little use and stopped using her sword. But before long the men succeeded in wounding the dragon and would have killed him if the other dragons had not come rushing to his assistance, then Chrysothemis saw that her strokes were of use after all and began using her blade more vigorously than before, and many a king's man that came to tackle in real earnest that captain dragon was wounded in the leg. At last the remainder of the king's men were sorry that they had tackled Sarbea at all, and all ran away except seven which went into the dragons' stomachs. Not one of the latter were slain and only one of Sarbea's men.

The dragons' wounds were bound and not many days after they were as well and strong as ever. Sarbea was exceedingly proud of them, for he knew that after his day had passed they would guard the pearl for years and years, the dragons that could not die a natural death. The next thing they did was to go into the labyrinth and visit the pearl, and Chrysothemis was fascinated by its beauty and colour. She too was indeed satisfied with its safety.

They build a cottage, and, though from time to time people from a neighboring island make a raid on the pearl, the raiders are swallowed by the dragons, so that the two lovers live in comparative peace. Chrysothemis is happy in her garden and her freedom; often she lies on the ground to admire the blue sky. Her own many jewels are placed in the labyrinth, under the surveillance of the dragons. One extraordinary episode is recounted in this connection:

One pearl she was very fond of, for her great-grandfather who had been a sailor as well as a king had fished it out from a great oyster shell that he himself found. The shell as well as the pearl she had, but the pearl she treasured more. She left it in charge of the captain of the dragons to guard beneath his tongue. And keep it warm. And indeed there must have been something magic about this extraordinary care, for one day, as Chrysothemis was going into the labyrinth to see the pearl a little snow-white bird flew out of the dragon's mouth and nestled in Chrysothemis's hand. For years she kept this bird and then it layed a single egg and died. This egg looked just like Chrysothemis's pearl, but even if it was it had some extraordinary magic about it for a week later there came a dove out of it who in turn gave birth to an eagle. The eagle helped defend the captain dragon, but the enchantress dismissed the spider, and cleared out the room which was now practically filled with webs, and made the dove keep the pearl under her wings. A few days later the captain dragon lifted up his tongue before Chrysothemis and lo, there was her pearl, just as it had been before.

The story of *The Great Labyrinth of Sarbea* has been left unfinished. In the remainder, written some time after the interruption caused by Barbara's inspired rebeginning of Eepersip's adventures, a number of raids on the labyrinth are described. A band of robbers, coming over from the neighboring island, are disposed of by the dragons and Sarbea, who kill most of them; but four of them manage to escape, and incite a wicked king to propose a reward of five million dollars and the hand of his daughter to any youth who might succeed in taking the pearl. Young adventurers swarm to the island. One comes with a monstrous three-headed lion. All are defeated, however, until there arrives one who has had the foresight to provide himself with an enchantress. He anaesthetizes the dragons that stand in his way with a magic liquid, threads the maze of passages and doors, and comes at last to the pearl, which he takes away to the wicked king for his reward—a wretched reward for him, since, having once seen the pearl, he cares nothing for the millions of dollars or for the king's daughter, who marries him out of cold obedience. Meanwhile, Sarbea and Chrysothemis discover their loss:

Then he sadly lamented and said: "Ah, miserable man that I am. How wicked I was to go away from my own country at all. The enchantress will kill me for losing her dear dragons and if I had never come here I should still have the pearl. Would that I had buried it with my poor mother and father." Chrysothemis shared his grief, but as they flung their arms around each other they heard sounds and rumbling noises, not looking Sarbea felt a strong arm grasp his neck and Chrysothemis felt the same, and turning suddenly they saw the captain dragon with them and all the other dragons rising.

A few more lines, most of them stricken out by Barbara's editorial pencil, indicate that Sarbea and Chrysothemis are on the threshold of further adventures, never to be written.

On comparing this story with *The House Without Windows*, one sees that Chrysothemis plays a role not unlike Eepersip's. Chrysothemis too leaves a father and mother, retires to an uninhabited rural spot, and there lives close to Nature in a garden full of flowering trees and thousands of millions of butterflies; and she has some of Eepersip's ethereal quality. As a further parallel, the love between Chrysothemis and Sarbea corresponds to an episode of friendship between Eepersip and a little boy. But the male in the labyrinth is a sexual mate rather than a friend, and the swords and the dragons, the labyrinth and the pearl, the woundings and the deaths, are charged with a chthonic power of a different order from that in *The House Without Windows*. For Jungians, the design of the labyrinth with its inner treasure room and four inner doors leading through a tangle of outer passages and past dragons to a hundred and twenty outer doors, also dragon-guarded, would certainly qualify as a mandala, or archetypal symbol of individuation, uniting chthonic powers, the psychic quaternity, and the central treasure ("the pearl of great price," which is the soul), and thus signifying Barbara's strong need to reconcile opposites and achieve selfhood on her own energetic terms. The Eepersip story, in contrast, is a flight from all the heavy darkness, materiality, and violent, unfulfilled desires which torment human mortality.

The contrast may be illustrated in another fashion by two poems in *Fairy Gold and Other Poems*, a booklet written, typed, and bound by Barbara and presented to her father with the dedicatory lines, "*To Daddy, on his Birthday, 1925.*" The title poem, "Fairy Gold," is an Eepersip poem. It goes as follows:

> I was lost in a meadow of fairy gold,
> Gold of butter-fairy-cups.
> The sun was setting,
> The flowers closing,
> Night was falling swiftly over all.
> A dim red light on the horizon
> Marked the path of the setting sun,
> All else was dark and darkening.
> The forest of pines, those tall and stately giants,
> Was shown against the rose-like flame,
> Burning like a rose in the dream-fire.
>
> The air was a-flock with tiny wings,
> Delicately fluttering.

All Fairyland was here—I saw it well,
As the little wings came closely snuggling.
The world was like a flower-bell.
The wings were its clappers,
And from a lonely forest tree,
Came the echoes and the tinkling.
A peal of silver music from the pine.
And notes, delicate as a butterfly, came following—
Winging their silver way over the trees.

The fireflies were glowing,
The earth was like a star,
And tiny insects were its sparkling points of light.
The wings crowded closer and closer around me.
I was buried in flowers, faintly fragrant.
The moon was rising,
A globe of soft silver light.
Around it played—quivering and shimmering,
Beaming, smiling rays—the fairies of the moon.
And then—or was it a thought?—
I'm sure the moon did smile at me!

The fireflies darted through the grass,
And there was a faint rustling, like butterflies' wings.
It was the fairies again.
They had left me, and, with flirts and rustles like silken dresses,
They fluttered about through the moonlit air.
The earth was like a dream, or a mirror of dreams,
And all of Fairyland was pictured there.
Then a flash of light passed like a mist before my eyes.
The sun was shining brilliantly.
It was daylight, and the cowslip meadow
Gleamed—a mass of fairy gold!

Just preceding this poem, and unique among those in the collection, is one entitled "Immanâla," which expresses the other
direction of her mind, the direction of the great labyrinth. It
reads:

O, thou black beast with the opal eyes,
Thou fearless beast,
Lying on the icy rock-ledge, with icicles and bubbling foam,
Thy feet leave no track in the snow when thou leapest.
Thine eyes are like moonstones, or frozen stars with hidden
    flames,
Dark—wicked, and shining in the dead of night.
Thou art a shadow of darkness.
Thou art Evil—a beast,
Or a haunting spirit of the night.
Thou art a picture, on a mass of soft, translucent green,
Jet black against the starry, deep blue sky.
And from thy blackness shine forth those fiery eyes.
Thou fillest the spirit of man with haunting, deadly fear,
And "When thou diest, thou diest alone!"

To return to the composition of *The House Without Windows.*
In a letter to Mr. St. John early in 1924, Barbara wrote:

I remember I wrote you one long letter on Farksolia, but now I
would like to tell you a little about how my story, The Adventures
of Eepersip is coming along. Of course, you know how she ran off to
live wild on the great meadow, but I don't believe I ever told you
about how she got a little bit tired of the meadow and one evening
saw the sea from a high peak and went there, to the sea. Well, that
is what she did in the fourth summer that she had spent wild. And
there she spent her time playing with the waves and the sea-gulls,
being in the water probably a third of her time. She spent five
summers doing this kind of thing all the time and in the spring of
the sixth summer that she had spent at the sea and the tenth
summer that she had spent wild she went to the great pasture where
the "steeple-bush made the air golden" and where it was fresh and
beautiful with the scent of sweet fern. This is what I wrote about
this pasture. "There were lovely ferns and nodding golden flowers
and the air was scented with the intoxicating fragrance of steeple-
bush, the steeple-bush which makes the air golden with smells." To
quote actually that is what I wrote. And there Eepersip got so wild
that she could receive messages from the fairies, and one day they

came to her clutching her dress and kneeling before her and telling
her that she had a sister, five years old, and her name was Eeverine.
And Eepersip went back to her old house and without mercy on the
parents she took Eeverine away, to live wild with her! And oh! I
love Eepersip so! I have suddenly been having quite an outburst of
Eepersip all of a sudden.

A poem attached to this letter, and addressed to *"my dearest
friend,"* gives some idea of the energy which drives her, whether up
into the ethereal realm of the invisible fairies or down into the dark
where the black beast of Evil dwells. Thus:

> May every single butterfly
> And every single bird,
> Bring you my love unbounded,
> Like a vast—vast sea.
>
> May every single bird that chirps
> Sing love from me to you,
> May every ripple of every river
> Bring you happiness and joy.
>
> May every silver rain-drop
> Bring you tidings from the water-nymphs,
> The water-nymphs so beautiful,
> The water-nymphs I live among.
>
> May nothing harsh or ugly
> Enter into your life, my friend,
> May everything bright and beautiful
> Come flocking with love to you.
> May your life be like an appleblossom
> Or a wild rose bud.
>
> May a ship loaded with butterflies
> Of blue and fairy golden,
> Come sailing to your port someday
> Each bearing love to you.

A year later, February 13, 1925, she can write to the same correspondent that the most important activity at the time is the process of correcting the Eepersip story. *"Daddy and I are doing it together. When it is finished, and copied neatly, we shall send it to the printer, and it may be—! Then I shall dance indeed. To have a book of mine—! Oh, wouldn't it be all so glorious."* The letter contains, also, a reference of a very different kind, and we catch a glimpse of Barbara vis-à-vis her peers such as we are not accustomed to, nor is she:

I am having a birthday party the fourth of March—a children's party. That is one of the things I have never had—I have always just had my "grown-up" friends to a luncheon and a clock-cake. But this time I am really going to have the rough, noisy, school gang of children that go to the same play-class that I go to. I like them, with all their rough ways,—they mean well. They are all about my age. One was born in March, on St. Patrick's Day, two in April, one in June, and the others are a bit older. So you see, we are quite well suited to play together, and we have pretty good times.

Another year passes, and in a letter to Ethel Kelley, March 15, 1926, she mentions that she is still working on Eepersip, *"revising it with Daddy."* She also mentions having posed for a picture with the English writer, Walter de la Mare, and encloses a copy. *"It happened this way: when he was here last spring, walking with me by the Brick Row Bookshop, someone wanted to take his picture. But he refused to have this done without my standing with him— to 'help him out' as he said."* She gives, furthermore, a detailed account of a mountain trip taken with her father during the summer past, which is important as revealing the source of a long passage in the third section of *The House Without Windows*. The letter's account runs thus:

I now want very much to tell you about my mountain trip—for I had one last summer as well as the summer before. This summer I climbed Moosilauke with Daddy. We climbed it on the Beaver Brook trail—that splendid trail up through the gorge down which comes rushing Beaver Brook in gorgeous cascades that seem, when you look up at them, as if they were coming from the sky itself. The trail is very steep—and tiring, if it weren't for the brook. But with that splendid thing to watch you never get tired. I felt thrilled all the way—thrilled with seeing it every few yards—seeing a tiny silver stream way up, and watching it grow bigger until it became one of those cascades, slithering down over smooth but down-hill rocks, whirling round and round in rock basins, edging cautiously along a shelf of rock, as if afraid, then plunging down a fifty foot drop again.

But when we climbed out of the gorge and were on the fairly level ground by Mount Jim (a rounded hillock of a peak) little white clouds came floating in, thicker and thicker, until, by the time we had passed Mount Jim, there was nothing at all except a few yards of wet trail and dripping trees, scudding pearly mist, rising and curling into fantastic shapes. So when we really reached the summit it looked like the rest of the mountain except that it was covered with brown, long, sedge-grass which rippled prettily in the breeze.

Four days we spent in this thick mist, and the third it snowed, later turning into sleet. Some of the nights a gale came up and howled weirdly about the old top house, with a curious mixture of high-pitched whistling and bass droning, sometimes rising into a shriek with an awesome and terrifying sound.

The fifth morning we would have to go down anyway, for our provisions were getting low, but we still hoped for a clear morning. And at first it was not exactly clear, but there was a faint purplish glow over on the eastern horizon, and the mist didn't look quite so thick. And, lying around on all the rocks, the cairns, the wood-pile, house, grind-stone, and trail signs, were frost feathers. Frost feathers! What a magic name! They were ferns, feathers of layers of frost with scalloped edges, and with the most beautiful delicate tracings all over them. They ranged from ten inches to so tiny that they could hardly be seen; some were round, like the inner feathers of a bird, and some long and narrow, like the long outer plumes. Oh, they were so beautiful, so beautiful—never in my life have I seen anything that gave me such inexpressible emotion! They seemed to cluster everywhere that they could find room, and sometimes were even delicately traced on the snow itself. And one of the cairns that

Walter de la Mare and Barbara in the spring of 1925

had a little hollow inside it, was entirely lined with them, like a fairy palace.

But while we were watching them, things were rapidly happening in the sky too. The mist would break open a little and then close again. Suddenly it opened for a moment on the west with such a view! First the low foothills, covered, like an Indian blanket with the colours of the red October trees, the sun striking them in a certain way, giving them a strange light—these hills fading into the lower Benton Range, with the colours more concentrated, these fading into range after range of blue, billowing mountains, until they met the sky. Some of the valleys were full of white clouds which were rapidly lifting, and others were overhung with big, massy ones which cast dark, uncanny shadows down below. There were lakes, too, lakes molten with the gold of the sun which was breaking out, and sending away the clouds, and when the mist closed in these lakes it seemed to stay longer than anything else, and could actually be seen, as if hanging in mid-air. It closed in. A long wait. Then another direction opened in the same way, and another wait —then more and more, the mist growing thinner, the sun striking through everywhere, the sky pushing its way free, until—all the way around it was open, the sky was clear, and deep, deep blue, while the last of the banished mist floated slowly up and disappeared.

We had to go down, and I was sorry, but when I thought it all over, I was glad not to see the frost feathers melt. They were still in the tip-top of their beauty when I left them—the warm sun did not even blend the little scallops along the edges of even the most delicate pattern.

Oh, they were the loveliest things I have ever, ever seen.

In *The House Without Windows*, where the same experience is used, it is no longer a case of "we," for Eepersip has no company at all but the snow.

The book was published the next year, and very successfully, going into a second printing before publication date because the original printing of 2500 copies was sold out. So she tells Mr. St. John in a letter dated January 20, 1927. Later we find her writing an appreciative note to a reviewer who had pleased her by taking heed of her phrase, *"daisied fawn."* A few months after that, she is answering a child of her own age who had liked her book, and she explains a little about the book and adds some words on more recent activities:

A great many things, especially in the third part, "The Mountains," I have seen and known myself. I have been among "frost-feathers," and I have watched them form out of driving mist which freezes on to the mountain-crags and is cut and carved by the wind. And I have been on Mount Moosilauke when the clouds broke away and the sun burst out almost exactly as I wrote it.

But all of part two, "The Sea," is my imagination, for I have never lived by the sea, and I don't know very much about it—at least, I didn't at the time. I believe I saw sea-gulls once or twice down at the shore somewhere. Since then I know a lot more about it, and I know that if I wrote "The Sea" all over, I should write it much better. Early this June, I went off to sea in a three-masted schooner, carrying lumber down from Nova Scotia, and going back there without cargo. We encountered all kinds of weather—calm, thick fog, clear, and high winds. I lived "rough," like all the sailors, and I picked up quite a lot about the sailing of a schooner, and I learned how to do things on board—and I saw how the sea looks when the fog is so thick that you can hardly distinguish the water from the sky, and how it looks in a gale, when the foaming waves are high. I wish I could have had that trip before I wrote "The Sea!"

Just now, I am having a great deal of pleasure writing a long pirate story. That, of course, has a lot of the sea and ships in it, all of which I picked up just from those two weeks off in the schooner!

With this, we see Barbara entering a new phase, a phase already foreshadowed by *The Great Labyrinth*, a phase of—but let her words to Mr. St. John in a letter of January 20, 1927, explain it:

Speaking about books—if I recover from a bad cough, cold, and hoarseness before next Saturday, I am going to speak over the radio from New York. I shall probably read a narrative poem that I wrote a few days ago. I am both trembling and singing—at any rate, my blood is quite curdled. The trouble will be beginning. Then, I

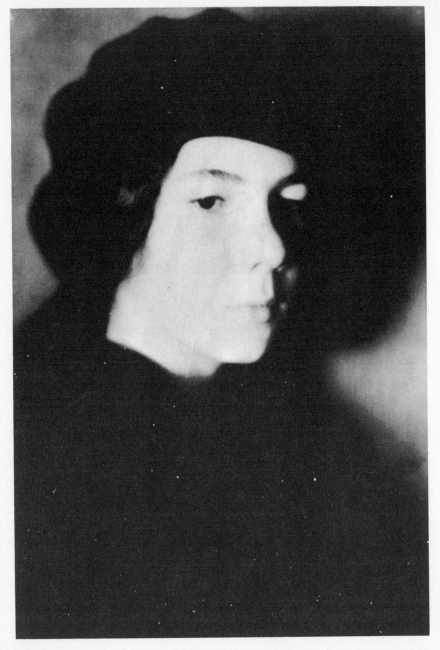

Barbara at about the time of publication of The House Without Windows (Stor
Studio, New Haven)

can't imagine how difficult it will be to talk and talk, and know that people are listening—yet just talking into a motionless, lifeless thing!

The narrative poem is like this: (You may think that I am very faithless to Eepersip and Nature, but, all the same, I am wild over PIRATES—their unknown islands, masses of blood-drenched gold, mystic maps, wild seas, wild fights, wild deeds!) It contains everything from Blackbeard to myself, from poppies to sea-shells, from butterflies to pieces of eight, from ghosts to living pirates, from maps to palm-trees. And, if you are interested in this (my first attempt at real rhyme and meter) I will send you a copy.

The poem lives up to its description. It is the Great Labyrinth brought to the surface of a real earth, made historical and richly detailed, and it combines and in a measure reconciles the fairies and death, the bright sky and the dark underworld. The operative element is a random cargo of poppy seeds hidden under the bands of the pirates' treasure box, which germinate in the grave where the box has been buried by the thieves and killers; so that the loot of the pirates is symbolized and revealed by the scarlet flowers which spring from it and flaunt their beauty over the whole island. This scarlet, beautiful life dancing over the grave of secrecy, cruelty, greed, and death corresponds to many an ancient thought, of course; but it is a thought which never wears out because its truth is rooted both in Nature and in the mind of man. Here in this poem is Barbara in 1927, approaching her thirteenth birthday and already halfway through her short life, crossing that mysterious divide between girlhood and womanhood, which, like the pirates' treasure, is marked with red—the red, not of poppies, but of blood.

"Poppy Island"

I

There are hundreds of isles among the seas,
    And scores where pirates used to go;
But only one in the whole wide world
    Where flaming scarlet poppies grow.

Like emerald glowing in azure and pearl,
   With winding flowery patterns of gold,
Lies Poppy Island; and even the gulls
   Muffle their wings, and cry "Behold!"

With crystal shells the sand is pearled—
   Foam-ridged sand, white and gleaming—
Cliffs dip down into azure and green—
   Gull-haunted crags, towering, dreaming.

Like falling trees in a mountain-storm
   Are the waves that topple and madly race;
The spray is high, the sea is snowing
   And edging the beaches with delicate lace.

The vivid, butterfly-luring green
   Quivers and rustles; the tropic isle
Spreads its arms to the smiling sky.
   And on their hill the poppies smile.

II

Dazzling, sunburned treasure lies buried,
   Sleeping, bright as sun on the sea;
Sleeping within a strong sea-chest,
   Locked with a jewel-encrusted key.

It lies there sleeping—sleeping, dreaming—
   Dreaming of pirates who left it there,
Dreaming of sinister lovers of gold,
   Each of them risking his life for a share.

It is buried high on a shadowy hill.
   Amid the sombre green and brown
There burns a banner of flaunting red
   To guard the place where treasure went down—

The brilliant red of waving poppies,
   Flowers to guard the pirate gold.

Strange, how strange! but this is the tale
    Of flowers, pirates, treasure they hold.

III

As a garden-box, the old sea-chest
    Rested once on a moss-smooth lawn—
The lawn of a garden glowing with sunset
    Of tulips, and poppies the colour of dawn.

But Blackbeard raided the sea-girt town.
    His pirates must sail with no delay;
And, richly laden with sparkling bangles,
    They spilled the flowers, and sped away

To sea, to sea! and the old chest too—
    Where ships talk softly, alone with the sky;
But poppy-seeds clustered between the bands
    Of the iron-bound chest—and they did not die.

It was Blackbeard's gold. The heart of that man
    Was darker than all his treasure was bright.
The great chest filled and filled with wealth,
    From many a raid and many a fight.

IV

Such treasure a pirate had never beheld—
    All taken under the Skull and Bones,
From many a gallant and goodly ship
    Sent calling untimely on Davy Jones—

Lustrous rubies, odd ingots of gold,
    Diamonds, garnets shining like blood,
Silver in waterfalls snowy with foam,
    Pieces of eight, like rivers in flood.

But the coins of gold! oh, the coins of gold,
    In dazzling, blinding fire-cascades!

Doubloons, guineas, moidores, and more,
  Like the island sun that never fades;

And more, and more, unbroken streams—
  Lakes, and seas, and mountains of gold;
The wealth of pirates that sailed the sea
  Is a fairy-tale, to be left untold.

But strangest of all their hard-won gems
  Were trinkets of delicate metal lace—
Fillets encrusted with opals and pearls
  That once surmounted some fair maid's face;

Bangles of pearl like fairy foam,
  Curious bracelets of golden spray,
Adornments like feathery mountain-frost
  Decking the wings of a dancing fay.

V

The chest was full. Blackbeard arose:
  "Now bullies, come, we must hide our duff
Where none but ourselves will ever go;
  Then beat up for more—ay, that's the stuff!

"Be sure to put no hands ashore—
  By the powers, I'll not be cheated again.
Mutiny follows, and all ill-luck,
  For putting treasure ashore with men.

"The last time, we marooned a man:
  And, swollen with revengeful pride,
He moved the treasure and covered it well,
  And gleefully then lay down and died.

"Take care, take care, lest this happen again."
  He gave five pieces of gold to each;
They lowered the boat, and muffled their oars,
  And landed the chest on the island beach;

Then over the vivid tropic glades,
    Over dank moss, to the shadowy hill—
Murmuring grimly, with cutlasses drawn:
    "Him who bothers this, him we will kill!"

By a ferny palm they buried it deep,
    And spaded and tumbled the thick clods on—
But how should they know of those other gems,
    The deathless seeds of the flower of dawn?

Then Blackbeard plotted his secret map,
    In vivid green, with the tree in red.
Long before night, with his pirate band,
    Away from that mystic place he sped.

VI

But the seeds were there, in twinkling clusters;
    And how those tiny specks of gold
Valiantly pushed the earth away,
    Thrusting up through the leafy mold!

Up they lifted their pale green shoots
    To the quivering sun of the southern skies,
And wondered to see the gaudy wings
    Of blazing tropic butterflies.

One scarlet blossom trembled there—
    Another—others; each fragile stem
Was crowned with its shallow cup of fire,
    And the hilltop grew alight with them.

Like a crimson dew the petals fall,
    Seeds shower down like golden rain;
And seasons pass. But where are those
    Who should come and find their gold again?

VII

Ah, where indeed? Beneath the waves
    Among the dead who tell no tales;
And nevermore need the Seven Seas
    Beware of them and their blood-stained sails.

But the poppies remember Blackbeard's men:
    The fire above guards the fire below,
And flies their colour, the colour of blood.
    Do they rest in peace, remembered so?

Their treasure is flaunted and betrayed!
    To the far horizon it stands revealed!
Can they lie still in their watery graves,
    With their richest hoard to men's eyes unsealed?

VIII

Now we will wait, and watch, and see,
    Behind thick shrubs on the shadowy hill;
Ghosts of those pirates are filing along:
    "Him who bothers this, him we will kill!"

Robed in the garments in which they died,
    Eyes still cruel, faces still brown,
Each has a cutlass clenched in his teeth,
    To defend the place where treasure went down.

Blackbeard still is in the lead.
    His tunic, as in days of old,
Is bound with ghosts of amethysts
    Set deep in reddest burning gold.

They look as once they looked in life,
    But make not even the ghost of a sound.
They gather about the old, frayed map;
    And now the treasure-place is found.

But when they see the poppies there,
    They huddle together in deadly fear;
They eye each other, as terrified
    As if the King of Hell were near.

Shivering slightly, Blackbeard turns,
    And speaks in a dreadful, ghostly tone:
"'Tis an evil omen, my bullies; come
    Away from there, and leave it alone."

IX

The dew is falling, deep, soft pearls;
    Dusk swoops down on the vivid isle;
Only the poppies stay, undimmed—
    Only the poppies quietly smile.

One by one, the pirate ghosts
    Vanish now in the budding dark
And, slipping through the blackened woods,
    Sail away on their ghostly barque.

I have told my tale of the Poppy Island,
    Haunted with gulls that echo the cries
Of "Gold!" and "Blood!" that once went sounding
    Shrilly through those windy skies.

Chapter V

Before publication of *The House Without Windows* the pirate blood had begun to boil, and in the summer of 1927 Barbara seized the opportunity presented by a three-masted schooner in harbor at New Haven to ship aboard as a member of the crew for a voyage, in changeable weather, to Nova Scotia. The vigorous letters written to a friend about her adventures were turned into a book, *The Voyage of the Norman D.*, published in 1928 by Knopf.

Except for the energy manifested, this was an entirely different book from the earlier one: realistic, detailed, humorous, salty with the sea, the rigging, and the sailors. The thirteen-year-old "cabin boy" scrambles daringly over the whole boat, up the mast, out on the bowsprit, down into the hold, and into the lives of the crew; and she faces the charm and violence of the sea with open, quivering nostrils, and a great violence of joy in herself. The book was less enthusiastically received by the reviewers than the previous one, but it put her in touch with a number of correspondents whom she rewarded by a generous outpouring of her rapidly mounting technical knowledge and her thorough appreciation of old ships and the characters of those who work aboard them; and she cultivated the friendship of these men of the sea, so much to her liking and so different from the academic people who had been her chief associates before.

But storm clouds were beginning to gather on land. The first intimations of her father's ultimate separation from his family were rising on Barbara's horizon. Within a very short time the storm broke. Since changing his editorial position from New Haven to New York, her father had been less at home, and by 1927 the periods of his absence had lengthened out. By early 1928 the unity of the family was clearly threatened. The essence of the story in its meaning for Barbara is contained in two letters, dated April 1927 and March 1928.

As prelude to these should be read a letter from a happier period, when Barbara was eleven and there was no hint of a rift but only the usual longing for her father when he was away. The date is July 18, 1925, the place "The Cottage in the Woods," New London, New Hampshire. The letter epitomizes a relationship which has already been variously expressed in previous chapters, from the "Mr. Horse" and "Daddy-Dog" of the earliest writings to the editorial companionship of the years of working on *The House Without Windows*; for this letter is from the period between the first draft of that book (and the fire that destroyed it) and the final published version. Eleven-year-old Barbara writes:

My dearest Daddy:

The lake is still very high—it seems to me that it will never quite get ahead of the rains—for, you know, there have just been two big rains here, of the middle-size—just the size to keep back the progress of the lake, and for two days, the lake has made no headway at all. These rains have brought lots of nice things, all the same. To begin with, there are lots and lots of mushrooms and bright fungi around in the woods—also lots of Indian pipes. I do love those odd little things. If I look around on the leaves it does not take long to descry a clump of those waxen white flower-fungi—for that is what they are. I am beginning to learn where they are in the most abundance, so that when you come I can show them to you right off. There is quite a cluster of clumps near the path and very near the cottage, as yet unmarred by the blackness which they begin to show before long. And I am learning where they are for another reason—the fact that I hope with your help to make a fairy ring of them in my bower—bordered outside with lady ferns. It would be very pretty, I think.

There is a little chipmunk around here. I think he has a hole somewhere near, and so I have been feeding him and trying to make friends. I have put a lot of bread and crackers, etc., around, and I have watched him take a piece, sit up, and eat it in the most business-like manner.

I have been collecting lizards again—the red ones. This wet weather has brought them out like everything. I have nine in a box now. They are great fun, and very pretty. I love the amusing way in which they walk, with the front leg—no, the hand, touching the leg of the same side. When you take one in your hand, they walk to the edge, and when you place your other hand in front of them, they hesitate a moment, as if puzzled that they have to begin all over again. Sister likes them, too—and loves to have me hold her hand and let one crawl on it. I guess she likes the tickling feeling, for she laughs and says "Wuzheeds" (lizards).

The rain has made everything stand out so clearly. The moss and leaves are so green, the dead leaves are such a wet brown colour. I really think it is more beautiful than when dry. Dainty dallabarda blossoms (I'm not sure about how to spell this) are peeping out from the brown leaves, pushing up their tiny white blossoms, and they look so fresh and dewy. And the white pines are so full of drops of silver water, all in between the needles—you know how lovely that is.

When you come, will you please bring the animal book—the Geographic animal book—that is, if you are stopping at the house on your way up. You will find it next or nearly next to the Holland Moth and Butterfly Books on the left hand side of the lowest shelf on the left hand side of the bookcase.

With love from
Barbara

P.S. I am longing to see you. Nothing ever happens unless you're here. I haven't been out to the raft since you've been here. I miss you dreadfully.

B.N.F.

To this she adds some ink-marks of which she writes in her own hand: "*You don't know what the above sign means, but nevertheless write it in the same position when you write to me. It is very magical.*" And this magical sign is inscribed the full width of the page on the back of the copy of the letter which is still preserved, with this underneath, which is presumably the translation: "*With love and love and love and* love *and* LOVE *and* L O V E," all in the personalness of ink and with the words growing larger in a powerful crescendo.

Two years pass, and we come to the long letter of April 29, 1927, written by the thirteen-year-old from New Haven to her father in New York, employing argument and enticement to draw him back into the intimacy of association symbolized by *The House With-*

out Windows, for which he had so recently composed the loving "Historical Note."

Dear Daddy:

It seems to us that New York must be a sort of Louis XI's palace, full of snares, temptations, pit-falls, traps, and everything else for enticing and entangling its helpless victims. But now we have a stunning excuse for you to come home:

"The Brat" has a habit of calling at least forty-one times when Mother is in the house, but if she knows that Mother is out, she will hold her tongue. So we have the habit of going out for a walk every evening, so soon as the aforesaid "brat" is in. (She usually, however, has time enough to call three or four times before we are out.) Tonight, having nowhere in particular to go, we wandered over to see what the back-yards of our rich neighbors have developed into. (They are getting to be unusually nice back-yards.) Then a stunning idea occurred to me, and with much difficulty I persuaded Mother to scramble up Mill Rock a little way, and investigate the woods. Besides, I saw a patch of something green up high, which promised mystery. So up we went. The green proved to be a mass of plants which looked like overgrown mint, but among them, and up close to an overhanging rock, a columbine swung two or three red-and-yellow buds.

A long time ago, I had seen columbine up there, but I had never been able to find the place again. This time, however, I land-marked it carefully, and tomorrow I expect to take it up (since it is not a very large plant). But things developed tremendously in the course of a few minutes. There were multitudes of plants with leaves something like the leaves of bird's-foot violets, but with small yellow buds. I shall watch them. Up still higher we came on to a grassy path, which wound up the ledges. There were high, leafing bushes with graceful streamers up there, on one of which hung a few clusters of a kind of dangling barberry. Down on the right side of the path

(Not a whole garden is so
lovely quite
As a prim path with flowers
on the right!)

were clumps of leaves which looked as if they belonged to some kind of bulb (long, narrow, pointed), and, on investigating, I found patches of iris growing wild there, with some of them already budded. It looks from the buds like a blue variety. I expect to help myself to some of them. Still farther along on this mysterious path, we came upon masses of white and purple violets, possibly the largest violets I have ever seen. But still farther along was the great surprise of surprises. It was a wall—a high brick wall, with shrubbery showing over the top, and a red magnolia flowering at the foot. Near it were clumps of still another bulb—pale green shoots, not well matured yet. I shall certainly keep an eye (perhaps two eyes) on them. But I have some clue as to what they are, and I believe they are some kind of lily. For amid the shoots was a dried stalk, surmounted with a withered, stiffened, brown flower-cup, which was the shape of a lily.

I intend to make a great many visits, basket and shovel in hand, to this veritable Eden-of-cultivated-things-gone-wild, and I hope you will come along

". . . up to the pig-sties,
    and sit on the farm-yard rails!
Let's say things to the bunnies,
    And watch 'em skitter their tails!
Let's—oh, anything, daddy—
    So long as it's you and me. . . ."

And there really are bunnies skittering their tails. We saw an adorable small-sized one, as we came down, who flickered his white puff-ball, and he skittered from bush to bush, crouching quietly and melting "Into the landscape."

The wrens have again tenanted the green bird-house. Sister was the first one to see them going in and out. Their songs are everywhere now.

The pansies are flourishing nobly. . . . lilacs are still budding . . . . seeds are coming up as well as could be expected. . . . daily I find new lily-of-the-valley shoots. . . . most exciting documents are pouring in from Brookfield Center way, including a delightful review of T. H. W. W., also a great many important hints on the subject of sunset-reading, which I have now come to be proficient at. The only thing I can think of at this moment that is not progressing, is my pirate story. That is because the time I would otherwise spend on it, I am now glad to spend digging out-of-doors.

I wish you superb luck on your writing (whatever it is), only I am sorry you couldn't do it here.

You will enjoy my new-found "Mrs. Derby's garden" up there in the woods. It is very like the woods in which we found so many wood anemones and violets and yellow adder's tongue, a long time ago. I always have remembered that walk: though I can't even remember how we got into the woods, or where we were living, I still remember certain anemone-carpeted glades in those woods, and how we wanted to pick them all. Now, with my new craze, I should probably want to transplant them all.

Sister is making such marvellous progress in her reading, that I am greatly delighted and proud of her. She picks out the words come, away, and, play, and run, anywhere in her books. I got her to copy "come away, come and play," from her first reader on the typewriter. This gives her a chance to learn the little letters. We try to do some every day. She still skips about singing: "It is, it is a glorious 'fing' to be a pirate king!" Tonight, as we went down the front steps, we heard: "Yo, ho-ho, and a bottle of 'er rum!" with a terrible accent on the "rum."

We do hope you will tell us where you are staying. If Sister should dance out the window tonight, or should be wafted away like Persephone, we couldn't tell you of it until————Monday morning!

All good cheer to you,

and it is signed with a cryptogram for her name.

Less than a year later, the idyll of childhood is over. A letter from her father, arriving on her fourteenth birthday, brings everything suddenly to a head. There are no flowers in Barbara's reply, but all the flowers that she and her father had seen together, and the snows of the mountains, speak through her sober, mature argument. The date is March 7, 1928.

Dear Daddy:

I did receive your letter, yesterday afternoon, and I read it (as you must suppose) a good many times before I came to any conclusion or conclusions concerning it. And now that I think I have, I feel that I must point out two ideas in that letter that seem like ill-concealed weaknesses, and that cannot help but make me suspicious. (1) Because you do not give any clue as to what your answer almost was, and especially because you call attention to the fact that you have given no clue, I am tempted to think that the answer you had in your mind was one that you are now ashamed to reveal. For, had the intended answer been the right one, why all this secrecy about it? . . . Aren't we ever again going to cross ranges of mountains in all weathers, or play about in Sternway, or steer a real windjammer through the seven seas, or take sailing-lessons from Mr. Rasmussen—as we once planned?

. . . How am I to believe that you don't feel any more the lure of The Maine Woods—the lure of that mountain that we have always had vaguely in our minds? This is the time of year when you are wont to have feverish spells of the mountain-lure—why aren't you having them?

After further detailed discussion stressing the fact that her father is ill and exhausted and being misled into a decision harmful to the family, the letter concludes:

. . . Consider Sister. Can't you see that she is not possibly able to grow up decently in the midst of this whirlpool? Why she will have to spend all her time struggling to keep herself from being sucked down into it, and, as you know, she can't quite swim yet. And, besides, you can see that she can't in any way get along respectably with only two out of the three of us. It wouldn't matter which two you picked, she needs the third—she needs us all.

. . . I depend very much on you, and I trust you to give another heave to the capstan bars, to get the family anchor started toward the surface again. After all, you have the strongest shoulders for heaving of us all! And really, you don't want the family anchor to remain forever on the bottom, do you?

The letter was of no avail. Barbara's father, alone in his craft, had heard the song of the sirens without taking the precaution of having himself tied to the mast in advance, and he did not return to Barbara's world.

The disillusionment cut deep and the scars were permanent. Much of what follows in Barbara's life, to her final disappearance, can be read as a reaction to her father's desertion of her. But it can also be read as a continuation onto the plane of action of what was already contained in the phantasies of childhood. The study of human lives can never be reduced to the narrow requirements of experimental science; it is impossible to have another Barbara, an exact duplicate of her up to the age of fourteen, but differing from that point on in having a father who remained faithful to her and who carried out the promised expeditions in the mountains and on the sea and gave his editorial help when she needed it. We cannot, therefore, exactly estimate the effect of the actual Barbara's loss of her adored companion. It may be that the course of events would not have been substantially altered if the separation had been fended off. Yet, whether the domestic crisis be interpreted as the cause of certain following events or as simply the culminating point of a dramatic movement inherent in her life, there can be little doubt that Barbara's emotions and some of her actions were polarized by it.

After a short time any attempt to appeal to her father was abandoned. Barbara rejected him, and, on the whole, kept silent about him. She threw herself enthusiastically into a cruise by steamer and sailing ship, in the company of her mother, to the West Indies and Tahiti. She kept detailed and passionate notes on the scenes and the people she came to know. On returning to the United States, she worked closely with her mother in the composition of her mother's book on the trip, *Magic Portholes*, published by Macmillan in 1932. The title was Barbara's. The trip and the writing occupied her from September 1928 to June 1930.

There was an important interlude from May 1929, the date of the landing of their five-masted schooner in the State of Washington (the *Vigilant*, sailing from Honolulu), until March 1930, when they boarded the freighter *Marsodak* in San Diego for Baltimore. During this period she cultivated the friendship of a family of California writers and artists and drew closer to a sailor friend, A., the second mate on the *Vigilant*. Once she confronted her father and his companion and had to endure their disapproval of A.—disapproval which she met with scorn. Also—an event of symbolical significance—for her sixteenth birthday, with the help of her California friends, she cut short the hair that she had previously worn long and often in pigtails. She refers to the hair-cutting as *"one of the best afternoon's works I ever accomplished—or perhaps ever shall,"* and thanks her friends for *"the inspiration to my failing courage, and their spiritual splicing of my main brace!"* (S.S. *Marsodak*, March 4, 1930.) It is noticeable that at this time she often refers disparagingly to herself. For example, in a letter of February 1930 to one of her California friends, she writes: *"Honestly, I'm no good! Haven't the gumption of a weevil in a biscuit—and don't particularly want to have, either."* And again in the same letter: *"Ye'd better be disillusioned about me right away. . . . Really, I'm not worth the respect of a mosquito."* Yet she adds: *"But I'm happy as I can be!"*

We have met this reactive happiness before in Barbara. In her story "Maireena," written at about ten, when the heroine's father is dying she controls her tragic emotion—by abrupt refusal of intimacy with those who want to comfort her, and by distracting "happy" activities with a girl friend and animals. In the end, she confides only in her horse, Starre. Back of that horse (whom Maireena addresses as *"the only one I have to love, and the only one that loves me"*) there is the ungrammatical "Mr. Horse" of the very earliest story, the rambunctious father-companion whose faults are cured by the Bunny's magical wand—very possibly the fictional counterpart of Barbara's own father.

Apparently, at the period we are now considering, when the father's inadequacies and absence are by no means fictional, Barbara discusses him very little with her mother. The reserve breaks down now and then in letters to her friend in California, a woman author, and on these occasions she expresses herself sharply for the most part. Occasionally a note of tenderness slips in, very, very quietly. For example, in referring to her pirate ballad, she glances at the old relationship (January 1930): *"Do any of your young folk's juvenile healthy-minded periodicals ever take long poems, or ballads? I wrote a grand pirate ballad a couple of years ago, which I was in love with then, and am in love with still. Vanity Fair once offered to take it, if I would cut it down in length, which my father wouldn't let me do.*" One of the next references to her father in this sheaf of letters to her California friend, who continued to hear from her till the end, is in April, after Barbara and her mother have arrived in Washington, D. C. There is a wry humor in this letter of April 7, 1930: "*Do you know anything about what has gone wrong with the alleged and assumed source from which the large checks* au mirage *were alleged and assumed sometime in the future to flow? If so, I confess to a mild sort of human curiosity on the subject. Also: do not reveal to the alleged Source the exact whereabouts of Us. Mother wishes this to be a secret for awhile. If the Source wishes to communicate, he (or It) may do so via thee, my shipmate.*" In a letter of April 28 she describes herself as "*hardly a person right now—I am more like a machine. Typewriting, typewriting, editing, editing, cooking, sweeping, mopping. . . . That sort of thing. And busy as the devil, every minute, though not about the same things! (I hope.)*" She reports the visit of a woman who had been keeping her little sister in their absence—her sister, whom they had not seen in almost two years; and she cries out: "*She talked a lot about my little sister, and made us all very homesick—made me want to send a telegram to Follett and say: 'Drop it, you poor fool—and come HOME!'*"

The first two months after their return to the East coast were filled with intense hard work on *Magic Portholes*, along with odd bits of typing jobs which brought in a little money. About her mother's literary accomplishment she comments admiringly (April 28, 1930): "*I had no idea she could pull off anything of the kind. It's full of light-hearted, humorous conversation, beautiful little patches of description, not too much; and—oh, well, there's just no use talking about it, that's all! It makes my own stuff sound dull, and heavy, and thick, and formidable, and sluggish, and thoroughly awkward and ridiculous.*" And she conveys something of the intensity of the effort, which seemed to both of them necessary as distraction and as a future source of income:

But it is heart's blood, believe me! I wish I could draw an accurate graph of Mother writing an episode. On one side of such a

[103]

graph would be the progress of the episode; on the side at right angles to it would be Mother's corresponding state of temper, in which high would mean very bad. Thus, the beginning of the episode would be very high, where she realizes that it's got to be written. That's the familiar stage where she sends me to Hell for not writing it. The temper remains about the same while she flounders around—then she gets an idea, and the temper drops abruptly to a very happy frame of mind, near the bottom of the scale; there it remains a short time—then difficulties galore are encountered, and the temper line shoots to the very peak of the scale, and the apartment is an accurate representation of the nether regions, for a while, varying in length from half an hour to two days; then the difficulties are worked out; and with another abrupt drop the temper-line returns to the frame of mind in which the universe seems to be her special oyster, and a very nice one.

To be entirely fair, I own that my own temper-line would have to be marked in such a graph, along with hers; and I think the curves would be more or less similar, though not quite so exaggerated. . . .

We may infer more about the pressure of this work, and about the association with her mother under circumstances which discouraged frank conversation, from a penciled note at the end of a slightly later communication to her friend:

Oh, G.D. this——writing!xx!x! It's doubtless "good" for me— but it's fiendish, devilishly, hellishly Hell; it tends to give me yellow fever to the nth degree; and I'd as soon drink ten qts. of codliver oil. And I cannot ever express my feelings on the subject—except to thee, my dear. And the pressure gauge reads "Danger."

The MS was by that time all but finished, and the pressure was relieved by a short walking trip through the Pennsylvania forests, after which she writes her California friend the most ebullient letter of the period:

Washington, D. C.
June 3, 1930

Bestest of Shipmates:

We came back, from three heavenly days in the state forests of Pennsylvania, during which we hiked in the sunlight and starlight, and sang for sheer joy, and didn't worry at all—we came back, I say, to find a stack of mail—pleasant and unpleasant—awaiting us here. The pleasantest was yours of the 28th. In reply, I shall say right now that before I knew you I never knew how delicious an occupation dish-washing was, or what an enchanting beverage cocoa was!

Yes, all is well with me. Not well, but also WELL. I am NOT daunted—I am NEVER daunted. I think I'm building upon a great rock foundation—something. I don't quite know what it is. A philosophy of life? A creed? Well, anyway, it's on a rock. Did you ever hear my favorite old negro spiritual: "I got a home in-a dat rock, Don't you see?"

I think it is just too grand about E.'s winning that prize. I shall look out for it on House Beautiful covers. Maybe that really means something, don't you know? Not knowing anything whatsoever about art, I can't tell, but seems to me it does. I also think it's great about P.'s going alone to Detroit. You are wise in deciding that way, and so is she. Between E. and me, it ought to be fairly convincing that whanging on one's own is a Damned Good Thing To Do. This won't be much, but it will be something—a beginning—a start-off —and the saltiest old sailor that ever lived had a first voyage once, you know!

I shall probably be in New York then. I hope to be. I have six chances to get a job there—six fairly good ones, I think. My idea of Heaven right now is a place where one can get work without hiking the streets to look for it! If anyone would put before my nose work of any description, I'd fly into it like mad. But things like that don't happen. One has to whang, and bang, and hunt, and explore, and suffer, and grow shields and javelins and such-like in the process. Anyhow, I'm going to get a job this summer, or else die; by which I mean that "Nothing but death shall stay me."

I didn't know, until May 16, how much I really enjoyed A.'s existence, and what a glorious safety-valve that correspondence was. When the steam pressure got up, there was no doubt what to do about it—"write to A." Anything I said vanished as though into the depths of the ocean itself, and I could rest assured that no human or inhuman being would ever trouble the waters.There never was a safer, solider, more rock-like person in the world!

Well, I'm going to write again. I feel it coming. The MS is

finished now, except for the tailest tip of the tip of the tail, which is being done tonight. Then we go to New York, probably day after tomorrow. When that terrific load is off my shoulders, I'm going to plunge into something. The outline of it—a Magic thing—is already mapped in my mind. Someday perhaps I'll send you a copy of that outline for your own personal consuming. Strange to say, it's not D. at all, but something rather different. It has ships and the sea in it, and an island where everything was perfect. And there are difficulties which are not overcome by suicides or murders, but by sheer strength. And there is a Jinx in it, discontentment; and there is a Betrayal of that island, which ruins it. It ends on a very minor key indeed!

What with It and with Farksoo, I think any time I have left over from the job-I'm-going-to-get will be thoroughly disposed of, don't you? And I believe I'm going to be happy as Satan himself. Great Jehovah! As long as you see that the whole thing's one damn tremendous YOKE (as my German second mate would say)—why, then, you are happy. The Great Trouble is that sometimes it becomes a rather cheap, low-down practical joke. But not too often. Besides, when it does that it helps one appreciate the lapses of— well, of Pennsylvania state forest, wood-thrushes singing at twilight, an orange moon setting behind pine trees, lonely little roads through the fragrant woods, wild deer flitting through the glades, laurel and lupine in bloom, and the sweet things that the woods feed you with, such as wintergreen and sassafras to hold between your teeth while you walk. Oh, Shipmate, when I got away alone into all that, my soul filled up with the wonder and beauty of it, fit to burst me; and I fell on my knees and said: "Virodine—an hour of this when the Joke becomes too mean, and I'll be happy forever."

And then I walked swingingly through the sunlighted needles and the new red-bronze wintergreen leaves, and I sang, and sang, in Farksoo.

Ach! I'm interrupted!

Your Shipmate,
Barbara.

A few days later, when the work on her mother's MS is definitely over and she is at a private address, alone, job-hunting, the subterranean murmuring can be more distinctly heard. Referring to her father and his companion, she writes, June 16: "*About the Parents. I know nothing about them, and I really don't care a damn now. I only care in so much as I sympathize deeply with the situation confronting you and E. when they came trooping up to the desert. It was—well, it was one of those Grand Accidents that Occur Occasionally. I don't particularly want to think about them. I tried sincerely to get myself to write, but failed of course. They don't seem quite of my world at present. I am truly very happy now, and I want to keep to this particular circle, for the time being at least.*" But one can be brave only up to a certain point, and it is not only the external relations of persons and places which are affected by external events. In the next paragraph of the letter she confesses: "*The only thing that makes me unhappy now is that my dreams are going through their death-flurries. I thought they were all safely buried, but sometimes they stir in their grave, making my heart-strings twinge. I mean no particular dream, you understand, but the whole radiant flock of them together—with their rainbow wings, iridescent, bright, soaring, glorious, sublime. They are dying before the steel javelins and arrows of a world of Time and Money. I am happy the whole live-long day—happy as a bird—but when night comes and I settle down in bed for a night's sleep, then my tortures begin. I don't know when I've had a night's sleep without a prelude consisting of an hour or so of writhing! By day I think it's a grand old adventure; by night I think it's Hell, and double Hell.*"

Another disappointment awaited her when she saw her sister again at last, after nearly two years of separation. She was now about six to Barbara's sixteen. Barbara writes to her California friend, July 18, of the reunion: "*About my sister. Please don't let your imagination go running away with you, or I'll die. You know, after all, she is only a little, little girl. It was almost a terrible experience, if you want the real truth. I rushed to her with my heart wide open, and my soul ready for the balm I felt she'd give—and the beautiful dream melted, and I found a little child—a darling little child, to be sure—who took all I could give, and gave almost nothing in return, because she could not, of course, and I was ridiculous to expect it of her, but expect it I did. She could not fill any need of mine—not the need I thought she could fill, that is, but something entirely different that hasn't got oriented yet; and the other need, the greater one, is still hungry. And it's dying now."*

A month later, August 18, the strain is evident, as she writes to her California friend from New York:

Have you Seen or Heard anything of the Farents? I confess to a mild sort of curiosity. I suppose I should write to them, but—oh my, oh my! You see, I feel that if I can stick out this particular present-minute, present-place situation, and get on top of it, and yammer at it, and smash it, and domineer over it, and be Snooty and Disagreeable to it, and Awe it, and just make it Cringe—why, then, I guess I'm doing all I have room for. And I am doing just that. So picture to yourself an Amazon, mounted upon a Bucking Elephant, and hammering that elephant over the head with a Fijian war-club.

Anyway, there's a picture of Joseph Conrad over this table. . . .

And NOTHING can daunt me!

"I got a home in-a dat rock."

Wings! I have 'em!

And Joseph Conrad sent me his blessing and his love. Not so very long ago.

And A. comes home in October.

Well!

Lots of things have Occurred to Me, anyhow. I think I'm ready to live a much happier sort of life from now on—I mean, to make the best of circumstances and of myself, and get a lot of pleasure and fun out of anything and everything. I wish poor Mother could do that as effectively as I have learned to do it. She hasn't. She's under water. God! And I can't rescue her. I do forty-nine fiftieths of everything that is done at No. 122, as it is; and I sing as I do it: "I got a home in-a dat rock, Don't you see?"

The proud stiff upper-lip trembles a little in the next letter, August 29, written from the apartment in New York while her mother i absent on a trip to New Haven. She says that she is fairly contented and anticipates the future as something possibly interesting. But then directly she adds: "*I think the masculine farent should be whanged on the head and wake up to find himself shanghaied to sea; and I think the feminine farent should tackle the first job she can light on. He isn't what you'd call a Man. He isn't half the man that some of the Dago workmen are down the street. He isn't halfway the man that Mate Bill is, or Cap'n Colbeth, or A. He should go to work and do some hard physical labor, under someone who can't be talked back to, and who doesn't care a damn for all the long words. Nothing could be better for him than to take a trip in the* Vigilant, *under old Captain Peasley, and first mate Jacobsen. Jove! He'd 'yump' around then, all right!*" And then, after the angry outburst, the tears flow or almost flow—but by way of reference to a play she had recently seen: "*I went and saw* The Green Pastures. *It is the loveliest, and most real, and simple, touching, glorious play I ever knew. Marc Connelly's negro play, you know. It interprets the negro's simple belief and religion. Lord God Jehovah is exactly like some kindly old white-haired preacher: he has a little office up in Heaven, and every morning two angels, with dust-covers over their wings, come in and dust it. The whole story is there from the beginning—Adam and Eve, Noah and the Ark, Moses, the pilgrims on their way to Canaan; and all through it the choir sings negro spirituals, most of them familiar—and you get to the point before long when you just want to lie down and weep.*" She recurs to this play and her emotions in her letter of October 4: "'*Green Pastures' is easily the most tremendous thing, in a dramatic line, that I've ever seen or heard of. I think it beats—for effect and appeal to one's innermost vitals—Hamlet, or R. and J., or any of the old stand-bys. . . . When Jehovah (a kindly, fatherly old preacher in a frock-coat) produced the firmament in a terrific thunder-clap, I wept and wept.*"

A more indirect but no less essential expression of her grief and resentment is her increasing cynicism about the world in general. She writes from Pelham, N. Y., June 16: "*I think, as always, that the whole great Thing we call Life is one huge practical joke, anyhow. If we take it as such, it is instantly powerless, and we may* with impunity exult. THEN––the old Joke treats us Well for a change, and we begin to forget that it is a Joke—with the result that we are unprepared for the next battering. Then is heard the rumbling, ironical Laughter of the Gods. I think a good, sound, healthy pessimism is a Wise and Noble Thing." In a letter from New York, August 18, the picture is grimmer: "We are just Victims, that's all. There are half a dozen or so great Wheels grinding around toward each other all the time, interlocking on the rims, and if we happen to get caught between them—we just get mashed." According to her testimony of July 14 from Norwich, Vt., the despair, though usually hidden, goes deep and is permanent: "I certainly don't think there is much to be said for this so-called civilization. It's barbarous, that's what it is. . . . But lest you think I'm becoming very despondent myself of late, let me assure you that this is my normal state of mind, when I allow it to come to the surface. That is, I always am grieved at the world. But I usually don't allow it to come to the surface. I sink it. And I do love listening to these hermit-thrushes. They are divine. And there are a few beings whom I love a great deal, and who make most of what there is of Good in life. But I don't believe in God. God got discouraged and gave up long ago, and I don't blame him, I'm sure!"

"I always am grieved at the world." That is evident from far back in her childhood. Her letter to Mr. St. John of January 23, 1923, when she was not yet nine, draws up her bill of particulars against the world. She is oppressed by human greed and cruelty and murder. To escape them she imagines Farksolia. Yet, paradoxically, Farksolia contains these same ills. The human imagination, Barbara's too, is corrupt. She seeks consolation in wild nature and finds it there, but the loneliness which haunts her is not dispelled. The reciprocity of love is what she needs. In spite of her distrust of the world, her disillusionment with her father, her dismissal of God, she still believes in love. The aching, inarticulate void demands it.

Chapter VI

The intellectual rigors of New England civilization made it difficult for Barbara to recognize or tolerate some of her deepest emotional stirrings. A certain reserve, almost a primness, marks the operation of even her imagination during the childhood period. Later, the intellectual control gives way occasionally before gusts of weeping, sorrowful and tender.

It is worth noting that few things moved her so deeply as Marc Connelly's *Green Pastures*. The simple religious faith expressed in this play, the vision of a Creator who can with a single thunderclap produce a universe and who is yet only a pure-hearted, kindly, patient, infinitely wise and loving old darkie pastor, somehow broke open her fountain of tears. Such trust and tenderness, so uncalculating and so unintellectual, struck her hard. On the whole, Barbara denies belief in loving Omnipotence from a very early age. God is enemy or fake or fiction; at any rate, not needed. *Green Pastures* caught her off guard; it crumbled her intellectual defenses and left her weeping. It must have been rendered all the more potent by its contrast with the day-to-day hardness of the life she knew in the offices and subways of New York, where she had to struggle for existence while disappointment with her father gnawed relentlessly at her self-confidence.

It is possible to find a particular reminiscence which may have strengthened the effect of *Green Pastures*. In December of 1928, while on the island of St. Lucia in the West Indies, in the course of that voyage to the South Pacific about which she helped her mother write in *Magic Portholes*, Barbara witnessed a living drama of faith on the stage of perfectly earthly reality which moved her as profoundly as *Green Pastures* and in the same way. The Catholic devotions of the poor shocked and shook her.

Before arriving in St. Lucia she passed through other ports, and the people and tropical scenery took hold of her, so rich and mysterious in comparison with the New England of her first fourteen years. The magic was beginning to work in Barbados, from which she writes, in a letter of September 22, 1928:

Some of the natives here live in a most primitive way—it is a great relief. They live in odd little dingy cabins back off the roads; they keep goats (oh, the goats are too charming for words: little snow-white ones, brown-and-white ones, black ones, mottled ones), chickens, and pigs (we met a man with a family of pigs, who said he sold the littlest ones for sixpence!); they raise corn and sugar-cane and yams and aloes; and they have a little bright bank of yellow and orange and pink flowers about the door of their huts. HP and I, walking on a small grassy hill over the sea, saw a child singing an incomprehensible, flowery little song, the only words of which that we could catch were: "I love the dover; I love the dover—" whatever the Dover is! HP suggested that the child had heard it in church, and substituted "dover" for "Saviour."

Of her first sight of Bridgetown, she writes, September 24:

It is the quaintest little place I ever saw in all my life. The masts of the curious little trading-schooners grow all through the town, as though they were palms; there are absurd little rickety-wheeled donkey-carts everywhere, and baby Eeyores drawing them, with their sage ears nodding; everywhere are women with huge baskets of fruit and meat on their heads, walking the streets, and selling their wares. . . . I saw in the midst of the town the most really good-looking negro woman I have ever seen. She was standing on the sidewalk, holding ten or fifteen strings of red and white beads over her arms; she wore earrings, of course, and had a white cap on. And she looked very wistfully into my eyes, as if to say: "Now then, mistress, won't you have a little something?"

At the hotel (Marine Hotel) she is impressed by the trees:

This is a fairly large hotel, with a noble old palm-tree just outside our balcony, and numerous other unknown trees and shrubs, fruits and flowers, butterflies and birds. . . . There is a curious tree outside our window—a variety of palm, I think, which grows just beneath the first one I spoke of. It has long, long, branches, and they grow from the bottom up, rather than from the top out, like a true palm. And those long branches are waving all the time, like great fans, with a slow, uncanny, Egyptian movement. The real palm, however, is a noble old tree. And how marvellous it is by dark, black against the sky, with stars caught in its silent branches!

A poem written in Barbados sums up the powerful impact of this new land:

Darkness and mystery.
The moon shining
Upon the white, deserted streets.
A heavy, rich fragrance
From thousands of tropic blossoms.
Leaf-patterns from the guava-tree
Upon the white coral pavement.
A palm against the sky—stately—solemn.

Look! Is there snow
Upon the little stone church-step?
No, only the moon.
Far off, a cluster of staring lights
Like an enormous crocodile of gold—
The Dominica, asleep in the harbour.

One last sage-eared donkey brushes past.
Are you really contented
Little grey philosopher,
Or are you only wise?
Who knows his quiet secrets?
Who knows what he is thinking?
Who understands those nodding ears?

Silence.
Only the countless, innumerable voices
Of cricket, beetle, cicada,

All blended in one shrill, chirping note.
They sing without pause or fall.
The island's heart is singing.

The white flowers are as white as moonlight.
The orange ones are fleeting phantoms.
The pink ones are the colour of the wind.
Mystery—singing silence—moonlit darkness.
Why?

Those two are whispering
Over the little white gate.
Why?
What are they saying?
Their voices lift and fall, in whispers;
And their cheeks are ebony.

Away in the wet fields.
A lone hut, dark against the sky.
Who is there?
No light—no voices—nothing.
Only—joyous music—
Music for dancing, music for gayness.
Where is the laughter?
Where is the dancing?

Music—and, in the darkness,
Shuffling feet. . . .

After two months of exploring the islands of the West Indies the
mystery still lies heavy upon her. At length, the human or human-
divine mystery is heaviest of all. It repels her, it goes against the
grain of her New England demand for reason and cleanliness; and
yet it masters her. In December in St. Lucia she records a part of
her experience in a letter to Mr. Oberg, her childhood correspondent, now rarely addressed:

The few (natives) who have not adopted modern costume

and customs seem to be the elderly women of high class—judging from their extreme nobleness of countenance and their cleanliness of dress as compared with the others. I have visited the Catholic church here several times, and I have a queer fancy that the only persons who really and truly belong are those fine, middle aged women. I sometimes step into the church during the afternoon before the evening service, just to watch. One of those gorgeous creatures sweeps along the aisle toward the altar, with a steady, slow, queenly gait. She kneels and prays upon the red velvet carpet. And she belongs. She wears a long, quaintly cut, flowing garment of rich purple cloth adorned with a marvellous pattern. This dress has a high neck and long sleeves, and a skirt which sweeps to the ground, and which is caught up on the side. Beneath it she wears a white petticoat trimmed with stiff lace, and around her neck she wears a bandana handkerchief of a plain colour. There are gold earrings in her ears, and she wears a red or blue bandana tied fancifully about her head. Really, she is quite noble and glorious to look at, as she sweeps up the aisle holding her rosary, and as she prays upon the red velvet carpet.

. . . .

I have shed bitter tears, standing at the back of the church. There seem to be services all day long, and the whole town seems to be there. Between services there are still many natives sitting there with their rosaries. I stood at the door one evening during vespers. A poor woman, with nothing but a few rags about her, passed along the sidewalk with a big basket on her head. She took off the basket, and knelt upon the hard stone church-step, knelt there all through the service. A dog came along the sidewalk, sniffed at the door, walked in. I held my breath. He walked up the aisle as if on tiptoe, and then lay down halfway up, and rested there through the whole service! Why?

Why do these people attend church all day long? Is it merely "something to do" in these peaceful islands? Is it fear of Hell? Is it actual piety? What is it that wrings their hard-won pennies from them into the collection dish? I have wept and wept about those pennies. I know just how hard-won they are, and what a penny means here to a native. For a penny one may purchase four big breadfruit. For a penny one may purchase a dozen oranges. I have watched these people dip their hands in the stoup of holy water, and cross themselves with it. And I know what vile, feverish water it must be by the time hundreds of people have dabbled in it. Ralph Blanchard has had actual experience of holy water visibly squirming with mosquitoes. Oh, how ghastly it all is!

And you should see the wayside shrines in these Catholic islands! There is one not far from here, along by a very muddy river. It is a sad little place of stone, in the midst of the cemetery; and within it —O God!—within it is a ghastly crucifix and pictures of Mary, with several other dreadful little images. Before these things are placed faded artificial flowers in dirty glasses. And the native women walk up those steps, take off their baskets, kneel for fifteen or twenty minutes before that shrine, and put their haypennies in the slot. Now, I don't condemn the images and flowers and crucifix. They are no doubt atrocious and even scandalous, but I don't condemn them. After all, these people have done their very, very best with them, and they mean something to them, it seems. I think the faded flowers very touching. I could weep bucketsful about the whole thing, anyhow. I saw one poor woman approach with her newly born baby in her arms, and, after kneeling, she rose and held up the baby, as if to show the holy Mary the very best she had to show. How touching—how ghastly touching—how uncannily touching it all is, anyhow.

The Catholic church in the town is a grandiose structure and very respectable, but there is another church near this shrine—a little hovel with a cross upon it. We went inside one day, H. and I. More little images, more faded flowers. H. approached the altar, but I could not bear to intrude. There was a sick candle burning in a dirty saucepan in a corner—there was the altar overhung with unbearable pictures of holy personages. Perhaps I am to blame but I feel dreadfully about such things. It is because I envy it so. As I said before, I should like to be one of those gorgeous Negresses, with their long dresses and their rosaries, who approach the altar in the town church, and kneel upon the red velvet carpet. Happy, happy, happy that they are!

Yes, I envy anyone who can kneel for a half-hour upon a hard church step, and rise feeling happier than before. I envy anyone who can contribute a haypenny, feeling that it moderates their chances for Hell. I envy the trust, the faith in the presence of these mysterious beings in the presence of a mysterious country where they wander about in white robes and play upon harps. . . .

Although she succumbs emotionally at moments to the drama of these lives lived on different terms from her own, she remains outside, disturbed but still critical. Months later, in Tahiti, her reserve is temporarily broken down—by a feast and a dance. But this conquest is in a different direction. The religious devotion of the St. Lucia islanders is conspicuously absent from the Tahiti episode. It is not a question of submission to a heavenly power and participation in sacrificial suffering, but of throwing off civilized restraints for the sake of bodily activity—a fuller and more primitive and more sexual activity than any she had previously known, but still in keeping with the dancing, swimming and skating of childhood. The fifteen-year-old Barbara recounts the adventure in a letter written on board the S.S. *Sonoma*, May 14, 1929. A part of the letter is the following:

As I watched them, clapping my hands to the music of four or five guitars, I suddenly remembered my friend Mere, sitting comfortably upon the porch of her house in Papeete. "I don't want go heaven," Mere said, a mischievous twinkle in her black eye, as she unfurled the ebonywaterfall of her hair. "I want to go hell. In hell—plenty sweethearts. In hell—have good time, sing, dance around the fire, play on guitar." There was truth in what she said. The Tahitian dances would have astonished St. Peter; but the Devil and his imps would have howled with glee.

Corie wore a dress of green with a full skirt. Her hair was looped back and adorned with a wreath of red and white flowers. She was the most wrigglesome dancer of them all, and fiendishly excited. Her eyes flashed fire—those usually placid black eyes. She displayed two rows of gleaming ivory teeth. Every once in a while she would utter a long, hilarious whoop of joy. As she danced, there was a feeling growing strangely upon me—an ability to see into the heart of it, to understand. I suddenly liked her dancing, envied it, felt the spirit of it surging like fire through my bones. The native passion was aroused in Corie to the utmost; she seemed tireless, eternal. The crystal beads twinkled about her strong neck, flopped upon her green dress, flashed forth sparks of blue and red fire like diamonds. Her teeth shone—and her savage, beautiful, barbaric eyes. . . . By Jove, she was beautiful! She had awakened out of her usual everyday lethargy and sleepiness; she was awake, and having her fun now, and in her glory; and she danced, she danced, the very soul of life, beating the drum of life, with nature, with nature, living and dancing and dying, close to nature, in the heart of things.

One of her sisters carried into the room a baby—a wee thing, blinking tearfully from the sudden glare of light. I cast loose from my safe moorings at the tables, and went to see the little creature. It was a blessed, fatal move. The guitars struck up in a burst of hilarity, Corie uttered an excited cry, seized my arm, and exclaimed "Dance! Dance!" It was a perilous situation, that! Dance, and make a fool of myself; or not dance, and make a fool of myself? In the bright course of a second I had thought the thing out; and instinctively I made up my mind. And beside Corie, in the centre of the flashing ring of native boys and streamers of leaves and flowers, I stamped and leaped, and clapped my hands with native ardour. And so delighted and surprised were they all that they forgave me for not participating in lizardian and snakesolian wrigglings. Oh, she knew life, did Corie; she lived close to it, and dealt with it primitively, just as she was intended to long and long ago. What a heavy brown arm it was that she flung across my shoulders, when we had finished! Oh, I was her life-and-death friend now, I had shared her emotions and her secrets; all barriers had been mystically broken down.

An immediate sequel to this mystical dissolution of the barriers was that one of the native boys offered to dance with her, but he was very drunk and she rejected him. A remoter sequel was an offer of marriage. It came while she was still on the West coast of the United States after landing from the *Vigilant*, on her return from the South Seas. In a letter to her California friend, she writes:

I received a four page document from my Tongan friend in Vauvau, in which the amiable lad proposed marriage to me in the true native

*fashion, and winded (sic) up saying that his heart was 'beating like
an earthquake.' Isn't that exciting? Rather a problem, though, to
know just what to do about it. Shall I go and keep house in a grass
hut in the Tonga Islands? I can't imagine myself doing it, somehow,
even though Fugamisi may be the son of a very high-ranking native
chieftain!*

More than a year later, March 12, 1931, she mentions hearing from
him again. In referring to two interesting pieces of mail recently
received, she writes:

*One came from my dark suitor in the Tonga Islands. In his quaint
English he expressed the opinion that it was a "poor world." The
other was from a half-caste girl whom I knew in Samoa, and came to
like very much. I thought she had by far the most personality—as we
measure personality—of anyone I met down in those outlandish
parts. At that time there was something in the air about her
marrying a white man—a wireless operator aboard one of the Navy
ships, I believe. That was two years ago. I was interested to hear this
time that it was still in the air—in fact, she is to be married in April.
I am a little distressed of course, because I don't like inter-racial
marriages, and can't help having doubts about the man. She has
great dreams of coming to live in the States. Poor child! A
Polynesian is a "nigger" here, you know. If only one could say those
things. But no—you have to be silent.*

Far more important than these romantic incidents, titillating as
they were, was the attachment Barbara formed for A., the sailor
whom she met on the *Vigilant*. He was older than she, and it may
be guessed that to some extent he took the place of her father. For
about three years they corresponded, exchanging letters sometimes
as often as three times a week. Barbara valued A.'s philosophical
outlook and his solid, dependable character. Possibly both of them
dreamed from time to time of marriage. The marriage question is
not uppermost in the correspondence by any means, in fact is only
hinted at occasionally, but certainly the tie that existed between
them was very serious. It was Barbara who finally broke it.

Their relationship began in the easiest, most natural way pos-

Barbara at fifteen aboard the five-masted schooner Vigilant, Honolulu

sible. Here was a young girl enthusiastic about the sea, and a seaman who happened also to be remarkably literate, and they were companions on a long voyage by sail from Honolulu to the United States. After docking the friendship seems to have taken on added significance, as something with which Barbara could challenge her father. Writing to her California friend, July 4, 1931, she refers to the clash with her father over A. in the midst of reflecting on the dreariness of her life in New York, separated from A. by a whole continent and often by leagues of sea as well:

But oh, oh, in N. Y. the moths feed on the wings of your soul. This is probably an unhealthy attitude, I know. But I do think the world is rather horrid. Most of my dearest friends seem to be in deep trouble, and I can't do anything about it.

Perhaps that is why I cling for dear life to A. He, with no tools and no material, has nevertheless made something most beautiful and real out of life. I don't know just how. But he is a rock and a shelter. I'll never forget or forgive WF's attitude toward him. That was mainly what caused the sharp and sudden break between him and me. It was unwarranted and ridiculous and mean. My respect for WF did its loudest blowing-up over that. . . . A. is a treasure.

Barbara's correspondence with her California friend is full of references to A., and we can trace the course of the relationship in some detail through these letters. Before shipping on the *Marsodak* for the East coast, she mentions him in a letter of about January, 1930: "*There's been six inches of snow in Seattle, and bitter cold; and this has prevented A.'s job from going through—yet. And, because he also is a sensitive individual, such a little spark fired off a long train just as it did with me. He's all balled up, about himself, which is the worst kind of balling-up anyone can have, as you know.*" In February she writes: "*A. is still at sea in the yacht. Bless his heart—he sent me a telegram when they sailed so suddenly that he didn't have time to write. Weather reports say 'gentle southerly wind'—this of course is all wrong for him—sails, ye ken.*" Writing from Washington, D. C., April 28, 1930, while working with her mother on the *Magic Portholes* manuscript, she quotes from some of his letters. Having referred to the haircut in Pasadena which had ended her pigtails, she continues:

While I'm on that subject, I believe I will quote from A.'s latest. I wrote to him from Baltimore, sitting at the saloon table of my beloved Marsodak, asking what would happen to me if I should cut my hair off (tactfully not saying that it had been done, you see!). And here is what I got back:

"It seems that I am called upon to remark upon two matters of some importance, if one can consider the matter of a haircut of any importance. As you are probably bobbed, and even possibly shingled by this time, there's nothing to do but yield with good grace, and submit a word of commendation upon good sense, and convenience, in place of an approving glance. Bobbed hair is really charming, you know, when it doesn't hang straight down like rope-yarn from an Irish pennant. As you assure me that yours is wavy and inclined to curl, we may count the tresses well lost."

In the next breath he springs the Arctic adventure, the absolute out-of-touchness with the world for four months, and the element of risk and danger—all quite unconcernedly, and in the same somewhat humorous and heavy literary style. He then professed great concern for my personal welfare. At that time there had been quite a tempest, financially and otherwise, and I sort of expected I should have to walk the streets any minute for any kind of labor I could find. During the crisis, I wrote to A. And he came back with putting his worldly fortune at my disposal, at any time, and with expressing great grief and concern over it.

"I only pray," he says, "it doesn't cast you into the day-laboring class. I've been in it long enough to know what it amounts to, and what its probable end is. The sort of existence that leaves a woman a slattern at forty, and a man a dolt. Or if they have some perception, leaves them with a sort of misanthropic cynicism, bereft of ideals and appreciation of life. . . . This must all seem very serious and dull, coming from me."

Maybe I'm prejudiced somehow, but I think knowing a person like this is a great adventure.

I could also quote ad infinitum from the letter which arrived just before that last one, in which he remarks that there is one thing I have in common with my father—"the tendency, or ability, to dream." Then he said that my dreams were "beautiful and sane," instead of being "distorted, perhaps through long suppression, who knows?" Then he became somewhat grandfatherly, saying that dreams would have to be put on the shelf for the present, under these entirely practical conditions. Then he charitably adds: "Sure! Don't I know? Haven't I sat on deck in the moonlight, and let fancy put on its seven league boots, and go roaming?"

He is very much in her letter of May 29:

A. sailed on the 16th, as per schedule, sailed right out into space. Look up Point Barrow on a map of the Arctic regions—that's the end of the route—then they turn around again and circle Alaska toward home—if they don't encounter a nor'-easter, or an iceberg, or the pack-ice. Before they sailed he sent off one dashing letter, of quite a different tone from what you'd expect of a person embarking on such a mean voyage. He described his own particular position aboard, half-way between sailor and engineer (there are four gasoline engines for sails and cargo, you see); and then he wrote several pages in mocking echo of the "tourist literature" on Seattle, concerning statistics and what-not. And then he seemed to run out of material, and said "Well, goodbye!" or words to that effect. A person like that sort of takes one's breath away, seems to me. Very startling and overpowering.

In her next letter she quotes him on some very tentative plans that Barbara and her mother had toyed with, and on the legal proceedings between her mother and her father:

In regard to China—I'll quote from A. "The news of the unsettled conditions prevailing in China comes as something of a relief, in so far as it affects any immediate emigration of the Folletts. Frightful place, China. I've been out there a couple of times, and always felt a bit silly riding in a rickshaw. Takes an Englishman in a top hat to carry the white man's burden, so called, with any degree of dignity. I suppose I am as observant as the average, but at that I failed to notice much in the European part of Shanghai that differed greatly from any city of equal size anywhere else. What novelty or glamour exists within the native quarter is more than discounted by strange sounds and bewildering smells. The American concession is more American than New York or San Francisco, and so it is with the British concession."

A. is distinctly a satirist. He says that he "can't understand why it should be continually necessary for lawyers to write 'final letters' to Follett." When I reminded A. of Helen's belief that A. considered her exceptionally sane, he replied that "the memory of it eludes me." A. is really about the only entertainment I have, you see: you have no idea how one must suppress and curb one's Self when living with Helen!

A month after the last letter from A. before his departure for the Arctic, Barbara writes her California friend, June 16:

To be a safety-valve is just a small item which is an automatic and natural part of a Friend, don't you think so? As for A., he has served my needs a whole year now, and a rest will do both of us good, I suppose—though it is a little strange not to be able to anticipate those pencilled, air-mail envelopes! I shall hear from him—barring accidents—about the first week in October. I expect he will show up on this coast shortly afterwards. It would be like him to do so. Besides, I flatter myself a little that perhaps my friendship did something for him, too. I think we were mutually very good for each other—let the Parents say what they may!

Do you realize that exactly a year ago yesterday I set sail from Honolulu harbor in my beloved Vigilant? I was rather glum all yesterday thinking of it. It hurt. I suppose it will be years before I go to sea again, and I may never even see that schooner. I suppose that I spent about the happiest month of my life during that sea-trip in her. And it lasted even during that week in port, when I took over the cabin-boy's job, and when Helen, A., and I had cherry- and ice-cream-parties in the cabin after everyone had gone ashore, and when we used to walk up into that virgin forest two miles up the road, and eat salmon-berries. Life was beautiful then.

A.'s absence during the summer made the hard life harder. In a letter of June 26, she says: *"The more I see of everybody in general, the more I know that there are a few simple, quiet souls (like A.) who unconsciously and entirely unmaliciously knock everyone else into so many bedraggled cocked hats."* In one of July 18, though she is very busy in New York studying shorthand, writing synopses of books for Fox Films, and typing, and thinks that the crowded, rushed, tense life of the city has done her good (*"I feel more of a sympathy and understanding for People in General than ever in my life before, because I am One of Them, which I never was in my life before. I find myself buying my chewing-gum from a cripple in the street, rather than in a drug-store."*), she nevertheless adds: *"I keep holding out my arms—I mean my spiritual arms—like an amoeba or sumthin. A ceaseless need. Sometimes I think it's the sea, and sometimes I think it's A.'s correspondence, and sometimes I think it's just space I need, and the wild. And I can't have 'em!"* On August 1, it's: *"Then, too, it won't be so very long before A. is home, and I believe I could go through anything with an occasional letter from him to keep me going. I never realized before how he and I have gotten to depend on each other's support. We each have had such ghastly times! It's quite beautiful, I think—two hungry souls beating their wings desperately and finding such joy and strength in one another."* On August 18: *"And in October, A. comes home. And I'll have that fresh fuel for my Sense of Humour. Besides, I may earn a whang on the back from him, and that's worth anything."*

As A.'s expected return draws closer, Barbara's excitement mounts. A piece of news about the rescue of a trading-ship crew north of Alaska frightens her, until she discovers that it is not A.'s ship. In a letter of October 4, she writes:

I have set aside a few days around the middle of this month— marked them off mentally with red ink—for the days during which I may hear from my wandering sailor. Of course one can't tell—I might hear tomorrow, or I might never hear at all. Rather uncomfortable suspense. I don't know quite what would happen to me in that case, and I don't care to speculate. If I don't hear before

November, I shall be worried. I haven't many bulwarks. My family isn't a bulwark at all. You are, and he is. He is so simple at heart that he would be laughed at by some of this world, and distrusted by most of the rest—my farents, for example—my fermenting farents. He is the soul and essence of the sea. He can sit on a schooner's taffrail at night and become so utterly a part of the ship and the sea and the night that it makes you cease your breathing for awe. He is rugged and uncut, and, though so far above the standard of most sea-farers, he still falls far short, in some ways, of the shore-world's standards. He is ignorant—of the little things that don't matter. But he is so real that he puts to shame thousands of people who probably would consider themselves far "above" him.

And he answered a need of mine that nothing and no one else could answer, by knowing how to laugh, and by being serene and tranquil and deep as the trade-wind Pacific. Bulwark, oasis, anchor —what-you-will. Mysterious, too, in his comings and goings, as the sea with its tide. And a romantic soul. "Sure. Don't I know? Haven't I sat on deck in the moonlight and let fancy put on its seven-league boots and go roaming among the stars?"

He and Conrad would have hit it off grandly.

A.'s absence of more than four months has tended to dematerialize him and put him at such a distance that he can be examined almost dispassionately, though with a romantic heightening of his qualities. Very nearly Barbara has written his epitaph. But he returns. On October 11, at the end of a hard week at her first regular stenographic job, Barbara came home to the apartment tired and sick. A note from him lay on the window sill, where her mother had put it to surprise her: *"The truth must be told. It was more of a shock than anything else. Of course I had expected it for weeks, but my expectations were always naturally ended as soon as I came into the house from school and saw whatever mail there was. This time it had been your letter—a glorious treat. I wasn't ready for this that followed. It was like a terrific earthquake."* She answered the note at once, and then collapsed on the bed to suffer her physical pain for the rest of the Saturday afternoon and the following Sunday morning. And in her letter of October 13 to her California friend, she continues:

You can imagine, of course, how disorganized the poor man is. It was only a tiny note, just saying he had arrived. It was dated September 7—instead of October 7. That's a good enough illustration of what a long voyage of that sort does to one. He hinted, in a way that made my blood run cold—"the breeze of wind you suggested turned out to be a man-sized affair, and it threatened not to be all right for a while."

O God, these wild people of the sea!

Of course I can't believe it yet. It's been a terrible gulf. It will be a long time before things can be as they were. I had half expected that the threads would just pick up again where they broke, but threads don't do that. There have been too many vital changes. But maybe I'm wrong. Maybe I'm still stunned. And I still hear that "man-sized affair" howling about split spars and streaming rags of sail. I know!

When he gets more or less organized again—not before—I shall gently hint that we would both like to see him this winter. I have a good idea that he'll take the hint. It's very easy to ship coastwise, especially in the winter, and it's rather hard to ship anywhere else except offshore. I feel somehow as though we should have to talk and laugh before balance can be recaptured. I am all up in the air now. I have concentrated all my faculties on trying to believe that that little letter is genuine, and not some ghostly aberration come to haunt me. I felt as though I were writing to a ghost, Saturday afternoon.

Not yet a ghost in spite of all, A. soon re-establishes the old relationship. On December 13 Barbara writes her California friend: "A. and I commune continually; we nibble delicately at the earth as thought it were a piece of cheese, and we fool with stars as though they were a handful of beads. He (wise man!—) is hanging on to his job for dear life, while I stand by and approve. On the other hand, I hang desperately to my job, while he stands by and approves. Thus we get along, though it's very unsatisfactory not to

[127]

be together. I think he writes better and better all the time. His comments are really immortal." March 12, 1931, just turned seventeen, Barbara writes: "A. is marvellous. Honestly, I don't see how I could possibly get along without his twice- and sometimes thrice-weekly communications: all done in the best A. manner, and never less than two pages in length. He is—a rock." But in the same letter she has to add that A. will be leaving on another northward trip: "If A. were going to be here I should certainly make some sort of effort to see him, but he is going up North again, as perhaps I told you. Not such a long trip, he says, but I feel rather bleak about it. He is going because he wants the money and is saving it—For A Purpose." A letter of June 1 records his departure: "A. has gone, of course. . . . It was more of a jolt than I had anticipated. I feel quite nebulous, not quite sure whether I'm here." References to A. are scanty in the succeeding letters during the months of his absence, but in October Barbara writes: "In words, then, know that he has returned, and all's well. He has been writing to me in his usual dear, faithful way, and between us we've just had the Airmail-envelope presses going to their full capacity. He is one of the world's best, I think—and if other people don't think so, they needn't, and you can tell that to the farents, and be damned to them!" A December 22 letter says: "He remains the best thing that I can see in life. (See???) It's his steadiness and strength and complete trustworthiness that makes him stand out so, in a complicated and discouraged world. I won't do any quotationing now, because I haven't time, but sometime I will. In the meantime, oh, thank God I've got him!"

But a new development was taking place in this "meantime" about which the letters to her California friend reveal nothing—except in retrospect. During the summer of 1931, while vacationing with her mother in a cabin in Vermont and working on her story, Lost Island, Barbara met several students from a nearby college. Among them was a young man, S., who shared her enthusiasm for nature and life in the open. With S. she resumed the mountain hikes that had formed so strong a bond between herself and her father. Upon her return to the city in the fall, S. frequently came down to see her; and, along with other friends, he and she eventually began to plan a long summer hike down the Appalachian Trail from Maine to Georgia. Barbara's letters to her California friend first mention S. in connection with these plans. It is in March of 1932 (she is now eighteen) that she announces the prospective summer adventure:

I've gotten together a party of four congenial brave souls—of which I am one (I hope)—and we may add two more members. Then, starting about the middle of July, we're going to Maine— Ktaadn—Thoreau's country—and from there we're going down the Appalachian trail, two thousand miles, Maine to Georgia, camping out, and carrying upon our sturdy backs the necessities of life. It will take between three and four months, and be the greatest release imaginable.

. . . .

The party consists of an amiable lad with occasional unsuspected depths whom I met last summer when H. and I were living in the Vermont cabin; a pal of his, who has a remarkably good head on young shoulders; and a girl who is really a grand scout, with whom I get along quite beautifully. In fact, we all get along with each other beautifully. No friction anywhere, as far as we have been able to discover. There may be two others added to the Grand Expedition, as I said; and we would like of course to have an elderly leader, than whom no finer could be imagined than M. of Hanover—only I'm afraid M. of Hanover is tied up.

Well, that's the general idea. It may crash completely. Nothing is certain about it. But we're all hoping, and pulling together. We're all slightly rebels against civilization, and we want to go out into the woods and sweat honestly and shiver honestly and satisfy our souls by looking at mountains, smelling pine trees, and feeling the sky and the earth.

Further along in the same letter she remarks: "All this time I haven't so much as mentioned A., have I? Well, I've had him in the back of my mind—in reserve, so to speak. Luckily, the (ship) job holds. I guess he'll be going north again next summer—the third time. There really isn't anything else to do, with conditions as they are all over the world, especially along the waterfront. His life *is odd and stern—verging on tragic, at times. He feels that now and then, and has down-spells, during which I am hard put to it to be cheerful and cheering. I am pretty sure, though, that next fall we shall actually be together, and discuss everything from moths to meteors, including money and mice and merriment and misery and —but that almost exhausts the m's that I can think of at this Moment. That discussion will doubtless decide a good many points about this universe and the nature thereof. Right now he is a little sad, and alternates letters about the futility of life with humorous epistles about politics in Seattle and other things."* On May 31 she writes another letter about the Appalachian Trail plans, saying that in June she is going to spend a week end in Hanover with old friends and shortly after be off on the trail; and in the midst of all this bustling news, there is a hushed reference to A., now almost a wraith: *"Yes, A. went north again. He is now first mate of the schooner, and rather happy about that, of course. He is doing awfully well, considering everything. I MAY see him next fall—but don't you breathe a syllable about that, even to yourself! I'm keeping it a very strict secret from myself. If you know what I mean. I mean there are some things in this world that don't happen if you so much as admit that they're possible. Perhaps they sometimes happen if you keep your eyes tight shut and don't think at all."*

And then there is silence, on him and everything else, for four months. At last, from Moosilauke Summit Camp, October 4, 1932, comes a penciled note referring to *"the curious, joyous upheavals my life has undergone, and the gypsy like ways I've been living,"* and concentrating in three sentences, without defining details, the essence of the summer past: *"I've jumped the whole structure of what life was before. I've jumped the job, jumped my love, jumped parental dependence, jumped civilization—made a pretty clean break—and am happier than for years. I've a new and I think a better structure of life, though time alone can tell that!"* Translated, this means that the Appalachian Trail plans had fallen through and that Barbara and S., defying the conventions, had lived together among the mountains and lakes of New England as children of nature, alone. Barbara had resigned her job in New

York, discarded A., broken off communication with her mother, and attempted to replace the rules and perquisites of society by the promptings of instinct, for the sake of the earth and the sky and the intimate company of one young man.

Chapter VII

Barbara's precipitate summer adventure established a human relationship which lasted, with ups and downs, for seven years. It also ended the romance with A. The three years of communion with him had inevitably raised a question which Barbara was reluctant to face and which was clearly among the topics beginning with "m" that would be up for discussion in the fall of 1932 (*"money and mice and merriment and misery and—"*) when, as she expected, they would be together. The marriage question would have to be settled. The summer alliance with S. settled it. By October she could say to her mother that a letter received from A. was unreal: *"The unrealest thing I ever saw. It simply doesn't exist."* Late in October she left with S. for Spain.

The end of the relationship with A. was not so abrupt, however, as the evidence of the letters might make it seem. In imagination, in Barbara's story *Lost Island*, the possibilities had undergone their maximum flowering and decline; and she had put the manuscript on the market before joining S. for the summer. The outline of it had been in her mind at least as early as June 3, 1930, when a letter of hers to her California friend described the essentials of the plot, and she was engaged in the writing of it from that time until June of 1932. Yet Barbara's intense correspondence with A. continued unflaggingly through that period as if her imagination had not told her that the end was in sight from the beginning.

In one sentence, the story of *Lost Island* is this: There was a perfect dream which could not last. The heroine, Jane, finds life in New York unendurable. Her work in the office of an entomologist is dusty and unreal, the city is repulsive with its meaningless speed and efficiency, and her friends have nothing to share with her but their frustrations. On a sudden impulse, arrayed in a flaming red skirt, she boards a sailing ship and leaves New York behind, bound for an unknown port. A close understanding promptly develops between her and the literate second mate, Davidson, whose favorite book (like hers) is Conrad's *Lord Jim*. A storm overtakes them in the Pacific off the coast of South America, the ship sinks, and Davidson barely saves Jane in a little sailboat which the captain whimsically kept on board. They are driven alone to an uncharted tropical island, nearly dead from bruises and exhaustion. There they find themselves in a sort of paradise. After a short period of physical recovery they strip off the last remnants of civilization, their clothes, and live in poetic intimacy with nature and each other. Davidson carves for Jane a marriage ring of ebony, bearing in relief two bounding porpoises, an anchor, and a butterfly. After three years they are jarred from their perfect happiness by the arrival of a scientific expedition which chances upon their island. The desecration immediately begins; a scientist to Jane's horror shoots down a bird to add to his collection, and the discovery of a gold lode dooms the island to eventual exploitation. Jane and Davidson, penniless and in rags, return on the scientific ship to New York. The monstrous city engulfs them. They adjust to it, and also to the painful realization that their economic need will force them apart, as she goes back to work in the entomologist's office and he on ships. Jane's old friends find her again. One in particular, a young man from Maine with an inherited income and literary aspirations, takes her dancing and makes love to her assiduously. She surrenders willingly to his attentions. But she feels divided in herself between her earnest, awkward sailor and this gay dancing companion who has a passion for the woods and mountains to match her own. Dissolution of the bond with Davidson resolves the conflict. The island is thus betrayed in two senses: by the murderous greed of a commercial and scientific civilization, and by Jane's capitulation.

The complexities of *Lost Island* are too much simplified in this account. The ending, especially, is more ambiguous than a scanty outline can declare, for it exists in two versions. Furthermore, it is not clear to what extent the second version was to replace the first or exactly how it was to be spliced into the rest of the manuscript. It is a further complication that we are dealing here with a 1934 revision of the original 1932 manuscript; it may be that Barbara's experiences with S. in that interval have altered or colored the original story and made it less purely a commentary on her relations with A.

The earlier ending represents Davidson as making a last visit to Jane in order to tell her that they must resolve to part forever because economic strain would not allow them to keep up the relationship begun on the island. She realizes that he is right: "*You could not bring into this world a perfection briefly attained in another, and expect it to endure. And it was obvious that to marry him would mean throwing them both into relentless circles of strain and worry, over each other as well as over materialistic things. He would be constantly in fear of failing her, wondering whether she was conscious of being failed, always aware of his worldly shortcomings, wondering whether he was imposing beyond reason on her love; and, most important of all, continually torn between her and her eternal rival, the sea.*" The final scene is romantically pathetic and indecisive:

He took her in his arms for the last time, and sat stroking her hair. She belonged to him still. She would belong to him always, only soon she would stand, a precious goddess, fragrant as wild roses, on some high pinnacle, inaccessible and remote, his own and yet lost to him, given to his ideal.

She herself was back again on the starlit hill in flower-scented grass; and a pang of hope made her wonder why this could not happen always, even in a shack in the slums, or anywhere else, why could not being together make the island come true, all the rest of their lives? But then she knew that would be asking too much of magic. It would rebel under such a burden; it would resent being called on, year after year, to be dragged through the dirt so that they might go on dreaming.

"David! Kiss me, and go quickly."

She was trembling a little, and he felt like a traitor. "I'd be even more of a traitor if I stayed," he said.

"Good luck to you, sailor."

He kissed her on the lips again, softly. "Maybe," he said, "it's lucky I'm a sailor. We're forever getting shipwrecked, or buying little boats with our last pennies, and bumming round. And somewhere there might even be. . . . The old sea has secrets still."

The later version does not give the last word to Davidson, as above, but to Jane. Or, rather, it is not a word she is given, but a long series of reflections bringing her back to the grim challenge of New York. The separation is an accomplished fact, and: "*She remembered how she had cursed the world, hated the world, screamed at the world for driving Davidson off from her—for driving him off into the clean wide seas on an endless quest. In a way the victory was his, for he had not compromised with love. He had taken the iridescent essence of it in the palm of his hand, sorted out of it every grain of earthly dust, locked it up and thrown the key into his ocean. His victory and hers—but at the price of all the happiness in life.*" Her consolation is in the Maine woods where the trees and flowers and animals calm her. Above all, the forest teaches her that she is alone and that everything is transitory. As she meditates she clings to a pine tree:

She looked straight up at the sky through surges of silver-green. Big bright clouds rolled by smoothly. She stared at them a long time, and then felt the swift sensation that she, her pine tree, and all the woods, all the world, were falling slantingly. She held on and watched, and drifted more and more into the swinging illusion of the thing. She and the pine tree were falling through space together. It was a long fall, and an oddly companionable one. She laughed a little at that. Life was relentless, but there was nothing more it could take away from her. She clung to her tree, ruthlessly divested by life of an entire world—a complete paradise—but the magic had been, and it was hers—as much hers and as real as anything could be in a transitory earth where no one could entirely possess anything.

She continues to reflect on the impermanence of everything, and from her mountain top seems to be able to look down on all the confusion of feelings and opinions and complaints in the world below as if they were spread out in complex circular patterns, all of them equally true and false, all absurd. And then with qualms she thinks of returning to the city, to a dull job and unhappy people, where she can be of little use to anyone. But she feels stiffened in her courage by the tree; she feels that she might serve as a sort of tree for others to lean on in their need, as in fact she has done in the past. As for herself, she cannot get that kind of support from any human being. *"It was odd, and significant, that in her need she could turn only to the original tree itself—roots truly in the earth, branches waving in the sun!"* Nature, not people; realities, not symbols!

Suddenly, from overhead, came a rush of song—notes that were clear and cool as moonstones, trailing up to a cascade of opals. Into the song of that hermit-thrush had crept all the joy mingled with all the sadness of her thoughts since she had come out by herself into the woods. As if the bird understood. Sunlight glanced through the leaves. The woods were alive and breathing gently. She was a pagan. She was in tune with them. . . . Clinging in silence to the white pine tree, she closed her eyes, but the cloud motion went on. She fell softly through infinite space, while a hermit-thrush sang.

Jane returns to New York, to its trivialities and miseries and pointless employments, among friends doomed to superficial contacts, to a civilization going on from triviality to triviality in the firm pretense that it was eternal.

She had an odd sensation, then, as though, like the light princess in MacDonald's enchanting fairy tale, she had lost her gravity. It was incredible that she should come back from her kingdom outside the world—come back and be able, even painfully, to adapt herself to life on earth again. It was incredible that the earth should still exist. She and it both should have undergone some supreme transformation. Instead of which—here she was. She was conscious that a few floating ragged streamers of rainbow still clung about her. She must carefully strip them off now, and put them into the trash-basket. In a few minutes it would be time to sally out to work. And you couldn't go to a respectable job in a bookstore with rainbow rags drifting about your shoulders, or star-dust in your hair. . . .

[136]

Jane laughed again, but there was a gleam of danger in her eye. Sometime, not too far off, she would stage another rebellion. It would not be the same kind of rebellion, though. One could never repeat the real adventures. That was why so many people were unhappy, she reflected. They tried to go back and repeat the things that had made them happy before. They tried to retrace the trail and visit again the places where they had known their highest ecstasies; whereas, if only they had the courage to push on, forward, over deserts and swamps and glaciers, they would sometime make new discoveries as bright as the others, or even brighter, perhaps. . . . One good way to start a rebellion was to buy a red, red skirt. . . .

The rain surged down with a steady drone. Well, it was time to go to work. Couldn't hang about the window all day. She peered out once more into the gray. As far as she could see, not even a cat was out.

If, as seems probable, this ending was written in 1934 or later, then it constitutes a reflection not only on an imagined relationship with a sailor on a paradisal island but also on the fulfilled relationship with the companion of her summer adventure in the New England mountains. For she shipped with S. to the Spanish islands and lived a life of vagabondage in the caves and blue waters there (like Eepersip in the sea), and later in the forests and high mountains northward in Europe—only to return at last to Boston, to be cooped up alone in a rented room and in the constraints of small employments. That was at first. Eventually, sometime in 1934, she and S. were living together again in legal matrimony. The economic struggle went on, and gradually their standard of living rose and they were able to shift to better apartments; but Barbara's contribution to the struggle, stenographic and secretarial work, did not appeal to her. *Lost Island,* and other writings, remained unpublished. Her husband, more and more absorbed in business, had less time for mountain excursions with her and was increasingly absent from home on business trips to various parts of the United States. She began to invest some of her spare energy in interpretative dancing with a semi-professional group, and in the summer of 1939 drove with friends to California for several weeks of advanced instruction in the art at Mills College. At the conclusion of the course, she went to visit the California friend with whom she had corresponded since 1929. To her there, in August, came a letter from her husband which shook the world down around her.

Whatever dissatisfactions Barbara had had to contend with in Boston, it is clear that her husband had become the most necessary of human beings. Perhaps she herself did not realize how much she needed him until the letter came. With him as a dependable reality somewhere near the center of her life, she had reached out to repair some of the torn relationships of the past. From the commencement of their close association, when they were in Maine in the summer of 1932, and later in Europe, she had extended generous invitations to her mother to join them and share in their fun. Her mother did join them in Germany in the Black Forest for a while. After the legalization of the marriage in Boston, Barbara and her husband assisted her father and his new family in various ways in their Vermont home, and she came to regard her father and stepmother with a certain esteem and affection, though constrainedly. She admired her own sister increasingly. Still, the family contacts seem to have been infrequent and not altogether easy and intimate. She had a job, she had her own circle of acquaintances, and she had a husband. Until she took up the semi-professional dancing, her life was pretty completely defined by her job and her husband. There were no children. Her literary activity had come to a standstill.

Her feelings about her husband, as revealed in the letters to her mother and the California friend, were uniformly positive till near the end. Even at that time, she saw herself as the one at fault. From Moosilauke Summit Camp in Maine, October 2, 1932, early in the relationship, she writes to her mother:

S. wears well. I don't know anybody else in the world (at least of the male sex) whom I would want to be thrown together with so closely for so long through so many variegated adventures. We haven't even scrapped at all, which is rather remarkable, considering how constantly and intimately we've been together since July. I've never had such an enjoyable and satisfactory relation with anyone. We're going to chuck it clean, when we feel like it, but now it promises to hold out ad infinitum, and it's grand.

From Palma, Majorca, she writes to her, March 30, 1933: "*You have no idea how much fun it is to be married, I mean when you REALLY AREN'T. . . . We have agreed that the first requisite of a happy marriage is not to be married. S. introduces me as Mrs. with uncanny naturalness! Thoroughly delightful. We get along better now than when we were over there, as we get to know each other more and more. S. can still make me laugh before breakfast, and he still labors under the pleasant illusion that I am beautiful.*" Four years later she writes from Boston to her California friend, April 5, 1937:

Life right now is a very quiet adventure, though pleasant, at that.

I have been tangled up with thoroughly unsuccessful people in a world sense (i.e., the various members of my family!) so long that I guess I have developed a consistent pessimism on the subject. Anyhow, it is a welcome and happy relief to watch S.'s progress. A few weeks ago they gave him another raise; and now he is almost earning what can be called a "living wage"; though it is not yet so alive but what I must keep my own job, if we are to continue our present standard of living (car, occasional beer, week-end trips, and such rather fundamental pleasures). But anyway, he is making "progress," and he is still thoroughly absorbed and interested in the varied aspects of his job. That is pretty thrilling, and compensates to some extent for the fact that I am thoroughly bored at present with my own.

Again, July 20, 1937, she is all admiration over her husband's financial success: "*It certainly would be a joke if S. turned out to be a money-maker, even on a moderate scale. Whether the joke would be on me, I don't know. I think the real joke would be on the rest of the family. My family has so long been associated in my mind with financial failure. It is hard for me to conceive that one member of it—me—could even be associated with, let alone* married to, somebody who is going to be able to make a normal living!" Then, December 21, 1937, there is exciting news of a dream fulfilled:

Way back in October we were prowling around the region near Squam Lake in New Hampshire when our eyes lit covetously upon an old farmhouse on a hill—a farmhouse that was in quite reputable condition compared with most of the abandoned houses thereabouts. To make a very short story of it, we rounded up the prosperous farmer on whose land the house is just sitting idle, and persuaded him to rent it to us on the incredible and absurd basis of $2.50 a month—the altogether delightful basis, I should add! We were quick to cart up some old furniture from S.'s family attic, and place same upon the floor of the farmhouse. Follett, over in Bradford, Vermont, crashed through with the very important item of one kitchen range which he was not using. So we set up housekeeping—week-ends. And, as easily as that, we had our much-longed-for, often-discussed Place in the Country.

Barbara's satisfaction with S. still holds, November 1, 1938, in a letter to her California friend which details some of his merits. He is seen as a bright spot in a somewhat depressing human landscape. She had just been to New York and seen her mother and sister:

Well, I'm afraid I haven't anything very cheering to report from that quarter. Mother's health is none too good; she is having trouble with her eyes and her teeth, and occasional touches of arthritis (did you know that?—I don't think she's telling people anything about it). Added to that is the rather overwhelming fact that certain booksellers in New York City have boycotted her book. You see, although it hasn't a mention of politics in it, it does happen to be about the pleasanter aspects of life in the German countryside! I don't know what her plans are; I don't know what she's living on, but it is certainly disheartening to her and to all of us, after so many years of desperate struggle, to be no better off. She has lots of friends, though, and her book has made her more friends—among the few people who have seen it, that is.

My sister—to present the brighter aspects of the picture—gets to be more and more of a corker every day. *She is fifteen now, and getting a kick out of being just in between, neither a child nor an adult, so that she can, as she says, get away with anything at all.* When I contrast her with myself at fifteen, I am likely to weep and gnash my teeth with envy. *She is happy, well poised, gets along well with everybody, a good sport, and a grand person. Added to all that, she is a marvellous-looking kid. She has got her hair done with a permanent in the ends of it, so that it falls softly around her face and turns up at the ends—lovely. She gets invited everywhere, goes to lots of parties, and gets fun out of every situation; and I guess all in all she is a principal reason why Mother still feels that life is worth living.*

Needless to say I am worried about Mother, but that is a situation of such long standing that I seem to have gone a bit numb on it. You know how it is—you can't just remain at a high pitch of worry for years on end! The same with W.F. and M. What odd and tragic parents I have! And how I enjoy S.'s calm poise, and his "success" in general, by way of contrast and variety!

The earliest indication in the available correspondence that the marriage had any flaw is a reticent passage in a letter to the California friend from Mills College, July 9, 1939: *"S. is about the only one I know who has a job, likes it, expects to keep it, and is earning a modest living wage! If I can just hang on to him I ought to be O.K. Whether or not I can remains to be seen! This winter I had a bad spell, made a mess of things, and have some ground to recover!"* In August, while visiting her friend, she received the shattering letter from her husband. She hurried back to Boston. On August 17, after a harrowing trip and two nervous days at home, she wrote to say that she had not yet seen him, and to thank her friend for helping *"to pull me through what was, and is, the worst thing that ever happened to me."* On August 22, she relates that he returned on Friday after her arrival on Tuesday. And then:

Well, all I can say is that what we conjectured was truer than true— I mean, that about the hell only beginning when I got home—not ending. I am glad I had thought it over so hard. I am glad I realized the importance of self-control. You see, the thing is really worse than I had thought possible. There IS somebody else. Just how serious I don't know, and I'm not asking any questions. That's part of the self-control. I haven't uttered one single reproach, or anything that could be construed as one. I've just dug my nails into my palms and held on, and held on, and held on, till now I think I'm getting to be quite a woman of iron and steel.

Well, I think there is hope for my side—some hope. I know it will be a long, patient process that will take all my strength and all my intelligence for a great many months. I think it is worth it, and I am going to make the fight. I don't blame him in the least. He really thought I didn't care; only, instead of saying anything about it so that I could have done something about it before, he just kept quiet and everything slid and slid. But it's really my fault; I had it coming to me, I know.

I think I've persuaded him to give me my chance. He is a very kind person, really, and hates to hurt people. He hated to write that letter; that's why it sounded so awful. I think that, if I can really prove that I'm different, why maybe things will work out. He still doesn't quite believe, as he says, that a leopard can change its spots! He thinks that in a month things will be all wrong again. So I say, at least let me have that month! I think I'll get it, and I think I can win if I've got the strength. Just this morning he said something that made me feel sort of hopeful. I think he is a steady enough person, and a kind enough person, and also enough of an easy-going person, so that he won't go making drastic plunges if he doesn't have to; and if I can make a pleasant sort of life for him, I think he'll hang on. That's what I'm banking on, and I'm putting heart and soul into all the little things.
. . . .

So that's the situation. My young doctor friend, who came over to see me that awful first night, has stood by and encouraged me. I don't know whether I told you he gave me some sleeping stuff. Ever since S. got back I've had to take it every night. The days I can stand, because they are sort of full of little things; but the nights I could never stand without some kind of help in achieving oblivion!

In a long letter of August 28, after describing a week end on Cape Cod with him *"looking for some nice country in which some time to have a summer place"* (whether for herself or someone else, she is unsure), she continues:

We talked a good deal about things, and at one point the conversation got to the point where it was logical for me to ask right out whether he wanted to make a go of things. I had had the feeling up till then that he definitely did not want to. So imagine my amazement, my almost hysterical delight, when he said yes, he wanted to make a go of it. Right away he qualified it, of course. He said: "Don't get too excited about that; I'm not sure that I can." I said if he wanted to that was more than half the battle; with both of us wanting to so much, and pulling as hard as possible, I don't see how there can be any failure, really. Well, what he said gave me enough heart to keep up the struggle. I had hit a very low point just before that—a point at which it just seemed impossible to keep it up any longer. Now I feel that I can; and I feel that if I handle it right for the next difficult few weeks, or maybe months, I can still win this game.

Things are far from fixed, you understand, but they are improving a little. This morning, when he left to go to work, he gave me a sort of rough pat, which is absolutely the first gesture of affection of any kind that has come my way! I still don't know how much of a situation I have to cope with in regard to this other person. I still have no idea who it is, how much he has seen of her, how far the affair has really gone, whether he is still seeing her at all, or how it stands. I know absolutely nothing, and I still refuse to ask any questions. M. (she is now home, after a terrific trip, and has talked to S. once about the thing) has an idea that the other person may be trumped up—that he might have simply set his heart on our separating, and thought that telling me that might send me hurtling off in disgust or rage. He apparently talked to her a little bit about this situation, and she claims he didn't sound a bit convincing when it came to this mysterious person. It would be lovely to believe something like that; it is a great temptation. But I have resolutely made up my mind that I have something pretty desperate to face in that respect; I am sort of disciplining myself to believe just about the worst possible, so that if ever I find out it wasn't that bad, the discovery will just be a relief. Well, I just don't know, and I have no way of knowing. S. is the kind of person who may very well never tell me just what it was all about; and if he will only come back to me I don't much care anyway. That again is absolutely proof—to me at least—that I am a radically changed person. I used to be full to overflowing with silly little petty jealousies. Now that a real thing has come up, while of course I feel terribly hurt, nevertheless any feeling of jealousy I might have seems to be lost in the bigger thing —which is simply that I want him back!

. . . .

There's another encouraging thing that I haven't told you, because it's so intangible. A change has come over S., a little, in the last day or two. He looks a little different, more natural, less strained. He moves more in the old easy manner—not harshly, abruptly, angrily, as at first. And he sounds different—whether he's talking to me or to somebody else when I'm around, his voice sounds more natural. He's obviously suffering, obviously puzzled, and looks pretty downcast a good deal of the time; but the tortured note, and the tortured look, the terrible strain, the angry glowering, have pretty much disappeared. I think that means a lot, and it bolsters me up, too.

There was another letter, dated September 11, and then an interval of nearly two months. The next came from a new address, an apartment in Brookline, under date of November 4. It is short, and the middle paragraph is not encouraging:

In my last letter I told you things were going well, and I thought they were. They continued to go well for a time—at least I thought so, and I was happy, and decided that the worst part of the ordeal was over. But that was too easy. No such luck! I don't know what to say now. On the surface things are terribly, terribly calm, and wrong —just as wrong as they can be. I am trying—we are both trying. I still think there is a chance that the outcome will be a happy one; but I would have to think that anyway, in order to live; so you can draw any conclusions you like from that!

There were no more letters—either to her California friend, or, as far as is known, to anyone else. On Thursday, December 7, 1939, in the early evening, Barbara walked out of her Brookline apartment. She had about thirty dollars with her and the shorthand notes she had taken during the day. She was never seen again. Or, if she was, it never came to the knowledge of her mother or the Bureau of Missing Persons, which sent out a five-state alarm.

For a while it was believed that she had run away, perhaps to her friend in California, and would return. As time passed and no trace of her was found, it was hypothesized that she had assumed a false identity and was living unrecognized somewhere, perhaps in some distant spot. A sort of open letter was addressed to her anonymously through the pages of *The Atlantic Monthly* in May, 1941, on that hypothesis; it was written by her father, and it chides her through his tears. The most incredible hypothesis was that she was dead. Suicide? She seemed too vital a person for that. Foul play? She was courageous and capable of looking after herself—and there was no evidence. What, then?

Many years afterwards her mother, in re-reading *Lost Island*, was struck by the significance of the following passage: "*This running away into the woods had always been her favorite escape, from other people or herself, beginning with her childhood in Maine. The woods of Maine were very different though from the tropical island. There she had looked up into a wavering lattice of pine branches, sparkling silver in the sun. She remembered one day, alone and half-afraid, she had put her arms around a young white pine, leaned her slender body upon it, and felt at once as though she had a friend.*" How consistent it would have been if Barbara, on that December evening, had carried her loneliness northward to her friendly woods and mountains! A snowstorm may have embraced her, an avalanche rapt her away. Here we strike into a deep

The last picture of Barbara, as a stenographer in Boston

theme. Is *The House Without Windows* to be read prophetically? Barbara never lived far from the bright country of her imagination, even when apparently subdued to the drabness of a civilization she never quite accepted. Her outward life in some measure followed the plot of her stories. There is more than a trace of resemblance between her life with S. and the episode of the boy beside the sea in *The House Without Windows* which precedes Eepersip's final escape from the constraining, absurd circular patterns of human attachments into the high mountains. Can we be far wrong in substituting Barbara's name for Eepersip's in the closing scenes of that book?

At sunset she was again at the peak of her mountain. The sky was flushed with magic; a great cloud in the west became brilliantly fringed with gold and red-gold, the east was all submerged in a lilac sea, and a delicate laciness of pink trailed across the zenith. Sunset fairies alighted on the snow peaks: they were fiery for a moment, and all the great snow-fields were flaming. Then the colour faded to pink on the summits. But in the sky Nature still flung about her colours wildly—fire was in the zenith, the long bank of clouds was vividly fringed with red-gold, and there to the south it changed to caverns of shadowed pink and strange violet. Seas and bays and cloud islands formed out of it—seas of a strange greenish rose. Then one thrill and flame of gold spread about the whole earth; the snow at her feet was shadowy gold, and a pathway of it danced upon the air 'way to the horizon. It played upon each frost-feather; the eastern mountains were flushed with this soft gold.

And then, dizzy with the colour and the beauty, Eepersip fell asleep, her fingers clutching the rosy snow.[1]

It was not long after this sleep that Eepersip, dancing and floating and growing ever lighter, was surrounded and adorned by myriads of butterflies of every pattern and hue, and, rising into the air with them, vanished—a fairy, a wood-nymph. And it was prophesied: *"She would be invisible for ever to all mortals, save those few who have minds to believe, eyes to see."* [2]

[1] *The House Without Windows and Eepersip's Life There* (New York: Knopf, 1927), p. 145.
[2] *Ibid.*, p. 153.